Connect, Communicate, Convince.

Public Speaking for Leaders and Professionals

Copyright © 2023 by James McGinty

For permission requests, write to the Author, addressed "Permission Request," at the address below.

Bespeak
1/1 119 Neilston Road
Paisley PA2 6ER
Renfrewshire
Scotland.

www.mcginty.net

ISBN No 9798854410168

Table of Contents

Foreword

Being on stage in front of an audience is the best way to Connect, Communicate and Convince. Whether you are selling a product, service or idea, speaking confidently in front of a group of prospects is the best way to let them see what sort of person you are, hear your message and ultimately purchase your products and services or engage with your idea.

The following 10 chapters will give you the tools to ensure that when you do get in front of the audience every word, every sound and every movement will captivate your audience so that you do Connect, Communicate and Convince.

Chapter 1

Connecting with Your Audience

People buy from people they know, like and trust. It doesn't matter, whether you are selling a product, a service, a political opinion or trying to cast yourself in a good light at an interview, connecting with your audience is step 1 of getting people to know like and trust you. Once you have done that it is easy to Connect, Communicate and Convince.

Here are 6 things you can do to enable that connection.

1. **Eye Contact**
   Make eye contact. Look around the room and make eye contact with various listeners. This creates a more personal connection.

2. **Be Inclusive**
   Use inclusive language. Say "we" and "us" rather than separating yourself from the audience. This brings them into the experience.

3. **Authenticity**
   Be authentic and passionate. Let your personality and enthusiasm shine through. Passion is contagious.

4. **Participation**
   Invite participation. Ask questions, do polls, have discussions. Getting the audience actively involved deepens engagement.

5. **Humour**
   Use humour strategically. Tasteful, relevant humour can help audiences warm up to you and your message. Just don't overdo it.

6. **Listening**
   Listen and respond. Pay attention to verbal and non-verbal feedback. Answer questions thoughtfully. Adapt to their needs.

Eye contact

Making consistent, meaningful eye contact is one of the most important techniques for engaging your audience and delivering an impactful speech. Direct eye contact builds an intimate connection with listeners, keeps their attention focused, and conveys confidence, credibility and care for your audience.

As you begin your speech, make sure to scan the entire room and make eye contact with various audience members. Avoid the temptation to look down at your notes or let your eyes drift around the venue. Purposeful eye contact reminds both you and your listeners that you are in this together.

Once you launch into your content, hold the gaze of individual audience members for 3-5 seconds at a time before shifting your focus to another person. Resist the urge to stare too long at just one or two people, which can feel uncomfortable or aggressive. Make sure to share this eye contact evenly across the whole room.

Proper eye contact technique requires consciously avoiding common pitfalls. Many presenters succumb to the impulse to break eye contact due to nervousness or self-consciousness. But pushing past this discomfort is essential for holding your audience's attention while boosting your own confidence and delivery. For inexperienced public speakers, improper eye contact habits such as staring over people's heads or focusing on just a few friendly faces in the room often become ingrained. Be aware of these pitfalls and keep recalibrating to make direct, purposeful eye contact around the room.

Audiences read meaning into the eye contact techniques of the speaker. A lack of eye contact conveys aloofness or anxiety and erodes engagement. Aggressively staring speakers can seem threatening. Delivering a whole speech without lifting your eyes from a page or screen is a recipe for losing the room. Aim for the ideal balance of warm, natural, periodically sustained eye contact.

To forge the strongest connections, strive to make eye contact with distracted listeners in the periphery or the back rows. Breaking through to these tougher crowds demonstrates your care and command as a speaker. Occasionally you may need to break eye contact briefly to reference visual aids or notes. That's fine, but always return your gaze quickly back to your audience. If using a teleprompter, focus your sight just above or below the screen while turning frequently to look directly out at your listeners' faces.

Many factors like room lighting, group size and audience receptiveness impact eye contact, so you may need to adjust your gaze strategies. Dim lighting makes it harder to connect with people's eyes, requiring you to widen your scan. Large crowds mean pausing on each person's face for a shorter time before moving your head to sweep through more people. Unreceptive audiences may make sustaining eye contact more difficult, but it becomes even more important for winning them over.

Remember that proper eye contact demonstrates respect, care and sincerity. It sends the powerful psychological message that you are speaking directly from the heart to each audience member. Eye contact fosters understanding. It provides nonverbal feedback to the speaker and forges a humanizing "I see you" bond. This simple technique can make the difference between a presenter who seems stiff, anxious and disconnected, and one who is poised, compelling and impactful.

Inclusivity

Public speaking presents a unique opportunity to promote inclusivity and consider diverse perspectives. An inclusive speaking style encourages connection and understanding between the speaker and the audience. There are several important techniques speakers should keep in mind to ensure their message resonates with a wide range of listeners.

Firstly, inclusive language matters tremendously. Using "we" instead of separating yourself from the audience fosters a communal spirit. Gender-neutral terms, rather than defaulting to male centric or female centric words, ensures everyone feels represented. Providing translations or explanations for any field-specific jargon prevents excluding those unfamiliar with the terminology.

A speaker can also be inclusive by acknowledging and respecting diversity within the audience itself. Recognize that each listener brings their own distinct background, values and viewpoint. Scan the room to consider the full spectrum of ages, cultures and life experiences represented. Customizing examples and anecdotes to reflect more of these varied perspectives makes your message land with greater impact.

Inclusive speaking means carefully considering opportunities for representation. Spotlight traditionally marginalized voices through quotes, statistics and stories. Make sure the imagery and language used does not perpetuate existing biases or stereotypes.

Represent diversity not just in terms of race, but also gender, age, ability, sexual orientation and anything else you can think of.

Approach challenging topics with nuance and compassion. Controversial subject matter may evoke strong emotions like anger, pain or grief for marginalized groups. Tackle uncomfortable truths through a lens of understanding. A diversity of viewpoints can illuminate obstacles to inclusivity which persist and how we might overcome them.

Inclusivity means recognizing barriers to access, both during and preceding the speech itself. Venue location, cost, timing, language services and accessibility requirements like ramps, translators or sign language interpreters should all be evaluated. Promote attendance diversity through both outreach and accommodations.

On stage, be conscious of optics. Represent diversity through those chosen to share the stage and their positioning as speakers or honoured guests. Shared podiums signal togetherness, while segregated seating can inadvertently divide. Represent community partnerships through visuals like logos or banners.

Finally, cultivate a culture of inclusivity within the institution or organization sponsoring the speech. Represent that spirit of belonging, allyship and accessibility from the stage. Though words alone will not combat systemic inequities, speeches can affirm unbreakable bonds of shared humanity across all differences. We must recognize diversity as a source of communal strength.

Inclusive public speaking sets an example of equality, understanding and celebration of our wonderfully heterogeneous global community. Through language, stories and appeal to our common hopes, speakers can transcend division to touch each listener's shared essence. Every public address presents a new chance to foster that inclusive spirit.

Authenticity

Authenticity is crucial for effective public speaking. When a speaker is authentic, they come across as genuine, relatable, and trustworthy. Audiences can sense when a speaker is not being real. Inauthentic speakers appear disingenuous, distanced, and unreliable. Below are some tips for cultivating authenticity in public speaking:

- Know yourself.
  Authentic speaking begins with self-awareness. Understand your values, passions, and unique experiences. Share real stories and anecdotes from your life instead of generic examples. Let your personality and sense of humour come through. This allows audiences to connect with the real you.
- Be transparent.
  Admit if you don't have all the answers. It's fine to say, "I don't know" or "This is new for me too." Acknowledge if you've changed your mind on something. Explain your thought process. Don't pretend to be an instant expert. Transparency makes you human and builds trust.
- Show emotion.
  Don't be afraid to express genuine emotion like humour, sadness, excitement, or nervousness. Appropriate displays of emotion make you relatable. Use eye contact, facial expressions, vocal variety, and body language to convey how you truly feel.

- Speak conversationally.
  Avoid stiff and overly formal language. Use expressions you would use in everyday conversation. Share personal stories and off-the-cuff remarks. Pause for natural laughter or applause. This conversational style keeps your content accessible and engaging.
- Tailor content for the audience.
  Research the audience ahead of time. Include examples, language, and ideas tailored specifically for them. Reference their location, profession, interests, or shared experiences. Show you took time to prepare content just for them.
- Be spontaneous.
  No matter how much you prepare, things may not always go as planned. Be flexible to adapt your speech in the moment. Respond conversationally to distractions or audience reactions. Go off-script if inspired. These spontaneous, authentic reactions can enhance your speech.
- Focus on the message.
  Don't get distracted trying to sound smart or professional. Focus on sharing your message clearly and passionately. Let your knowledge and expertise come through naturally. Sincerity and conviction are more important than elaborate language.

- Own your mistakes.
  If you mispronounce a word, lose your place, or blank on something, just admit it and move on. Dwelling on mistakes makes them awkward. Quickly acknowledging slips feels authentic. Audiences empathize with your humility.
- Be yourself.
  You don't have to transform into a slick, polished performer. Audiences want to see the real you, flaws and all. Don't conform to expectations. Share your unique perspective. Let your personality and passion shine through.

Authenticity takes courage but pays off with audiences. When you are real, audiences recognize it and respond. By focusing less on perfect polish and more on being genuine, you give presentations that engage, inspire, and build lasting connections. What makes you uniquely you, is exactly what makes you an authentic, compelling public speaker.

Audience participation

Savvy public speakers know how to strategically incorporate audience participation to captivate listeners and drive their message home. Rather than a passive one-way lecture, participatory elements allow the audience to become active contributors in the speech experience. When done effectively, participation boosts engagement, retention and feedback.

The simplest version involves posing rhetorical questions for the crowd to ponder. Let key points land by pausing after questions like "Have you ever considered...?" or "What if we approached this issue by...?". Allow a moment for mental responses before addressing the prompt yourself. This quick break from delivery lets audiences reflect.

For more overt participation, have listeners raise hands in response to queries like "How many of you have experienced this issue personally?" or "Who feels this proposal would positively impact them?" Hand raising keeps audiences alert while gauging reactions to content in real time. Modify based on visual feedback.

Call-and-response techniques invite vocal replies from the crowd. Statements like "If this resonates with you, say yes!" elicit verbal affirmation of your message. Just be judicious with call-and-response to avoid veering into cheesiness. Keep it concise and relevant to the preceding point.

When appropriate, divide into smaller interactive sections via guided turn-and-talks with neighbours. Pose a discussion topic or question for pairs to explore together for a few minutes. This welcome breather engages listeners collaboratively before reconvening to share out responses.

Question-and-answer sessions offer a go-to format for participatory engagement. Field questions submitted during the talk or in real time via a roving microphone. To encourage substantive dialogue, remind the audience beforehand to frame queries rather than make statements.

Pre-speech prep enables smooth integration of interactive segments. Give clear directions on what you'll ask of the audience and when. Provide any preparatory context needed to participate. Build in transition prompts before pivoting to a new activity.

Anticipate how the live group may respond based on their demographics and attitudes. Adjust participation methods to suit the audience and occasion. Rowdy crowds may thrive on high-energy call-and-response. More reserved listeners may prefer anonymous written questions or small group discussions. Know your audience.

Poll the audience to gauge opinions and foster inclusion. Anonymous electronic or paper polls allow shy individuals to contribute. Report back results to validate diverse viewpoints. Just steer clear of controversial or personal questions.

Remember that participation should align with your speech goals. Don't incorporate activities just for their own sake. Interactive moments must enhance the audience's understanding and connection to the material. Participation for the sake of participation easily becomes gimmicky.

Wielding audience participation takes tact and agility but engages listeners in powerful ways. At its best, audience participation makes a speech experiential, tailored and collectively created. Strategic, thoughtful interactions between speaker and listeners can profoundly amplify impact.

Humour

Used well, humour can be a potent technique for winning over audiences and magnifying your message. Laughter releases tension, makes listeners receptive, and transforms a stale speech into an engaging experience. However, humour misfires can derail an otherwise serious talk.

Know your audience and align jokes with their sensibilities. Humour relies heavily on shared cultural references. Anecdotes, pop culture jokes, or political satire suited for one group may bewilder or offend another. Gauge age, background, and values when deciding if humour has a place in that setting at all. Read the room.

Choose joke topics carefully. Self-deprecating and clean (PG-rated) humour tend to be safest for general audiences. Racial, ethnic, or sexist jokes quickly backfire in today's social climate. Poking fun at individual attendees looks unprofessional. Make sure quips are good-natured, not mean-spirited.

Keep humour relevant to the topic at hand. Humour for humour's sake gets old fast. Use jokes strategically to make substantive points or illuminate concepts in entertaining ways. Anecdotes should highlight teaching moments. Leverage levity to reinforce messages, not distract from them.

Be sparing with humour. Season your talk with fun – don't overwhelm it. The more you joke around, the more audiences expect it. Landing a few choice one-liners with perfect timing has more impact than a stand-up routine. Leave them wanting more.

Mind your delivery and timing. Comedy relies on gestures, expressions, and dramatic pauses as much as the writing itself. Record practice runs to polish your timing and delivery of jokes. Pace, enunciation and flair separate good gags from groaners.

Develop a repertoire of go-to bits tailored to typical talk scenarios. Audiences love inside jokes and callbacks to humorous anecdotes. Running gags threaded through a long presentation keep energy levels high. Just avoid overplaying the same bits at every engagement.

Practice new jokes extensively before debuting them in high stakes talks. Vet untested material on trusted colleagues first. Abandon bits that don't land in rehearsals. There's no recovery once a joke bombs before a large audience.

Be ready to handle jokes that don't land with audiences. Inevitably, some attempts at humour will miss the mark or elicit only scattered chuckles. Resist awkwardly explaining a punchline when no one laughs. Pause briefly then simply move on.

Consider your personal comfort with humour when deciding whether to incorporate it. Only tell jokes if it comes naturally for you. Forced humour is cringeworthy. Authenticity has the power to sell a lame joke - or ruin a good one.

While risky, humour wields unmatched power to engage audiences and drive home messages in lasting ways. A presentation's dullest statistics may be forgotten, but that one witty aside stays with listeners. Laughter forges connections. With care and practice, humour can humanize any speech.

Listening

Masterful public speaking requires honing the critical skill of listening while you talk. Audiences yearn to be heard and understood. Savvy speakers constantly tune in to nonverbal cues and adapt their message dynamically based on feedback. Listening and speaking simultaneously keeps the audience connected and the speech relevant.

Start by listening before the speech begins. Greet attendees as they arrive and make friendly small talk. Pay close attention to pick up on priorities, concerns and attitudes. The more context you gather beforehand, the better you can tailor the talk to their needs right from the start.

As you present, watch for nonverbal reactions. Furrowed brows may signal confusion, while nodding heads show agreement. Lean forward to catch visual feedback from the entire room. Make eye contact to detect restlessness or disengagement. Adapt in real time based on the signals received.

Read body language and energy levels. Crossed arms may reflect defensiveness or scepticism. Low energy could mean boredom. Learn to interpret these cues so you can adjust tone, pace, examples and emphasis accordingly. Watching the room is just as key as speaking to it.

Listen for the mood in the spaces between words. Laughter, applause and vocal responses provide obvious clues. But even silence can speak volumes. Let dramatic pauses hang to leave room for thought rather than nervously rushing to fill them.

Make time to listen to questions. Build in Q & A sessions to understand concerns and information gaps. Thoughtful, responsive answers outshine prepared remarks. Repeat each query to ensure you fully grasp it before responding.

After speaking, connect one-on-one with attendees. Many will reveal deeper perspectives face-to-face than they would vocally in a crowd. Listen intently during informal interactions to uncover valuable audience insights.

Solicit feedback via surveys, reviews or conversations with organizers. Criticism may sting initially, but listener feedback makes your next talk stronger. Humbly welcome the input rather than getting defensive.

Listen introspectively to your own instincts and reactions. Reflect on moments when you felt disconnected from the audience. Analyse what resonated versus what fell flat. Internal clues offer priceless pointers for improvement.

Curb any impulse to "speechify" regardless of audience response. Rambling past allotted time or sticking rigidly to notes against the mood of the room frustrates listeners. Talking is not the same as communicating.

Anticipate given the audience, context, and your topic, where engagement may peak or wane. Listen extra closely during key points to ensure understanding. High stakes material demands higher listening diligence.

Mastering the art of listening while speaking immediately differentiates you as an adaptable, responsive presenter. It fosters the authentic human connections that separate truly impactful talks from merely competent ones. Listen as you speak, and each speech becomes a dynamic conversation.

Chapter 2

Crafting Your Message

The key to a great speech or presentation starts when you begin to craft your message. Getting this right will go a long way to enabling you to Connect, Communicate and Convince.

These 6 items will help you do exactly that.

1. **Identify your core idea**
   What is the singular, most important point you want your audience to remember? This provides focus for your message.

2. **Understand your audience**
   Consider the audience's background, values, knowledge level, and interests. Customize to resonate.

3. **Organise your message**
   Organize your message logically with an introduction, body, and conclusion. Use transitions to guide the flow from point to point.

4. **Use Examples**
   Incorporate engaging examples, stories, and facts as supporting evidence. This builds credibility and helps audiences relate to the message.

5. **Choose your words**

    Choose your words carefully. Use vivid but simple language. Avoid jargon. Word choice impacts clarity and emotional tone.

6. **Practice**

    Practice repeatedly to refine and simplify. Keep honing until the core idea shines through clearly. A convoluted message dilutes impact. Craft for clarity.

Identify your core idea

Developing a clear, concise core message is crucial when preparing a presentation. The core message encapsulates the main point you want your audience to take away. It helps guide your content, keep the presentation focused, and provide clarity for the listeners.

When crafting your core message, start by asking yourself - what is the one key point I want my audience to remember? Your core message should convey your central idea or thesis in a simple, memorable way.

To identify a strong core message:

- Reflect on the purpose of your presentation.
  What do you want to accomplish? What change or action do you want the audience to make after hearing your message? Your core message should align with your goals.
- Consider your audience.
  What information will resonate most with them? What details will they care about? Shape your message to speak directly to their needs and interests.
- Review your content.
  Look for the main thread that connects your ideas together. Draw out the key insights, conclusions, or solutions you will present.

- Synthesize your research into one overarching statement.
  Capture the essence of what you aim to communicate, boiling it down into a succinct sentence or two.
- Lead with impact.
  The core message should grab attention up front. Open strongly and memorably to emphasize the significance of your message.
- Be specific.
  Vague, generic statements are forgettable. Include details, facts, examples that make your message clear, credible, and unique to your topic.
- Focus on benefits.
  Explain how your key ideas directly help or impact the audience, so they care about your message.
- Use vivid language.
  Well-chosen words and phrases make your core message more engaging, compelling, and easy to grasp.
- Align delivery with message.
  Your tone, pacing, visuals, and other presentation elements should reinforce your core statement.
- Repeat the core message.
  Revisit the main statement several times during your presentation to reinforce it with audiences.
- Close by looping back.
  End where you began, tying the core statement together with your final remarks.

By developing a singular core message, you create a North Star to guide your presentation planning, keep you on track while presenting, and ensure your audiences walk away remembering your most important point. Follow these steps to hone your message, remain focused amid other details, and craft a presentation that successfully lands your core ideas and leaves a lasting impact. With a clear, well-defined statement at its heart, your presentation content connects, communicates and convinces, and sticks with audiences long after you finish speaking.

Understand your audience

Knowing your audience is critical when preparing for any presentation. Investing time upfront to understand audience demographics, interests, needs and expectations will allow you to tailor the presentation content and delivery for maximum impact.

Start by gathering basic facts about the audience - size, industry, job titles and responsibilities. This gives you an overview of who will be in the room.

Next, consider what the audience likely already knows about your topic. You don't want to present too basic or too advanced information. Gauge their existing knowledge level so you can build an appropriate foundation while still adding new insights.

Look at the organization's priorities and challenges. What matters most to them right now? What problems or opportunities are they focused on? Shape your presentation to show how it applies directly to their current situation.

Reflect on why they are attending your presentation. Were they required to attend, or do they have a genuine interest? This gives clues about their expectations and engagement levels. Mandatory audiences may need more persuasion.

Try to understand individual motivations. For example, an executive wants different information from frontline employees. Think about what each role cares about and address those interests.

Learn the company culture and norms. Is it formal or laidback? Upbeat or muted? This helps you adjust your tone and style accordingly.

Consider generational perspectives in the audience. Different generations have varying communication preferences. Boomers may appreciate printed handouts while Millennials may expect digital interactivity.

Define your audience personas. Group attendees into categories based on shared attributes like role, priority, interest. Prepare information suited for each persona.

Check your assumptions through audience research. Survey or interview a sample to gain direct insights into what they hope to get out of your presentation.

During the presentation, observe audience reactions. Are they nodding, taking notes, glazed over? Tweak your approach to re-engage them.

After presenting, follow up with attendees to see if you delivered what they wanted. Apply their feedback to future presentations.

Thorough audience analysis takes time but markedly improves your presentations. When you tailor the content, style and delivery to their specific needs, they listen more attentively, absorb information better, and walk away impressed by the relevant insights you provided. Don't make assumptions. Do the work to truly understand your audience first, and they will respond with greater openness to your message.

Organise your message

A clear organizational structure is vital for developing an impactful presentation. Carefully planning the flow of information and sequencing your points strategically will make your message more memorable and persuasive. Follow these steps to craft a compelling structure:

Start with an introduction that grabs attention. Open with an intriguing statistic, question, anecdote or quote that relates to your central theme. This draws the audience in right away and establishes context. State your core message upfront and provide a brief overview of key points.

Sequence your main points logically. After the introduction, move through your key points progressively using transitions like "First...Second...Next...Finally". Or categorize points using headers like "Problems...Solutions...Benefits". Grouping related information keeps the flow coherent.

Use the inverted pyramid structure. Present background and supplementary data first. Then highlight analysis, conclusions, recommendations - the most critical info. This allows you to build up to key takeaways.

Leverage the primacy and recency effect. People best remember information from the beginning and end. Place your strongest points first and last when possible.

Chunk content into digestible sections. Breaking the presentation into defined segments with headers keeps the pace engaging. Audiences tune out during lengthy, uninterrupted lectures.

Limit each key point to 5 minutes or less. Attention spans today average just 5-10 minutes. Discussing fewer points in more depth leaves a stronger impression than a shallow skim of too many topics.

Use visuals wisely. Graphics, charts, photos should enhance your narrative, not distract. Carefully choose supporting images that clarify complex points.

Reinforce structure through repetition. Return to your core message throughout the presentation. Remind audiences how points relate back to central themes.

Watch your pace and timing. Leave ample time for key content instead of rushing. But move briskly between points keeping energy and momentum high.

Leave time for Q & A. Following each section or the full presentation, pause for questions. This allows you to clarify, elaborate on areas they want to better understand.

Close with a summary and call to action. Recap major points and core message. End by sharing recommended next steps, providing resources, or prompting audiences to take action.

With planning and practice, the presentation structure becomes second nature. You can smoothly guide audiences through introduction, key points, supporting evidence, recap and conclusion. A strong organizational flow keeps audiences engaged, allows you to land critical messages, and makes your presentation more powerful overall.

Use examples

Examples are an extremely useful tool to incorporate into presentations. Relevant examples help audiences connect with, visualize, and retain new information. Examples make abstract concepts concrete and bring data to life through stories, use cases, and analogies. Follow these tips for maximizing example impact:

Use examples to explain complex ideas. Introduce an unfamiliar or sophisticated concept, then walk through a specific example illustrating how it works in practice. This demonstration helps simplify and clarify.

- Align examples.
  Tailor examples based on the industry, job function, or concerns of attendees. This instantly makes the content more relevant.
- Leverage case studies.
  Real-world examples from recognized companies make concepts tangible. Audiences pay more attention when they see ideas applied by brands they know.
- Mix numerical data with narration.
  Back up statistics with anecdotes and stories. This connects facts to faces and emotions that stick better in memory.
- Use comparison examples.
  Contrast one concrete example with another to highlight differences and build understanding. Comparisons help audiences grasp nuances.

- Anchor with analogies.
  Relate an abstract idea to something familiar through analogy. Connections to everyday experiences or cultural references make new information more accessible.
- Set up examples with context.
  Give background like where, when or how an example occurred before diving into details. Context helps audiences interpret and absorb the example.
- Focus examples on action and behaviour.
  Examples showing human skills, consequences, interactions, or choices are more engaging than passive settings.
- Drive examples toward a point.
  Ensure all examples clearly illustrate a specific concept, principle or action you want audiences to learn.
- Use engaging delivery with examples.
  Vary tone, explore scene-setting, and incorporate dramatic pauses when walking through examples. This brings them to life.
- Choose details wisely.
  Include telling details that reveal key traits and illuminate your point rather than overwhelming with minutiae.
- Manage example length.
  Use concise examples as you introduce concepts, then expand on a few with more in-depth case studies or stories.

- Repetition helps retention.
  Revisiting examples in different parts of your presentation compounds learning.
- Check for understanding.
  After examples, use rhetorical questions or interactive polling to confirm audiences grasped your point.

With thoughtful selection and presentation, examples become a presentation's secret weapon. Audiences listen more attentively, retain information better, and stay focused when concrete examples illustrate your central ideas. Vivid, memorable examples drive understanding and are one of the most effective tools for convincing and engaging any audience.

Choose your words

The specific words used in a presentation make a tremendous impact. Word choice enables you to clarify ideas, create emphasis, tailor tone, and craft compelling messages that resonate with audiences. Follow these guidelines to choose words purposefully:

- Know your audience.
  Examine their education level, expertise, cultural background and preferences. This allows you to determine appropriate terminology and style.
- Use common words.
  Simple, widely understood language makes concepts more accessible to broad audiences. Avoid jargon.
- Focus on nouns and verbs.
  Precise nouns and action-oriented verbs add clarity and keep things moving.
- Limit acronyms.
  Spell out any acronyms first before using the abbreviated version. Keep acronyms to a minimum to avoid confusing audiences.
- Use conversational language.
  Write as you speak to sound natural. Avoid complex, formal diction in favour of words you would use in everyday discussion.
- Address audiences directly.
  Use "you" frequently. This makes the content relatable and engaging.

- Vary sentence length.
  Short, punchy sentences pair well with longer sentences for cadence. Avoid long, dense blocks of text.
- Check word associations.
  Ensure words do not have unintended connotations or colloquial meanings that could undermine your point.
- Activate strong verbs.
  Verbs like "ignite", "empower", "unleash" convey energy and motion.
- Use caution with qualifiers.
  Words like "may", "perhaps", "potentially" can diminish your authority. Balance qualifiers judiciously with more definitive language.
- Reduce filler words.
  Limit use of filler sounds like "um", "uh", "like", "you know". Thoughtful pauses are preferable.
- Watch for errors.
  Check for misused homonyms, malapropisms and incorrect word usage which undercut credibility.
- Avoid loaded language.
  Steer clear of words with strong political, cultural or emotional undertones that may polarize audiences.
- Repeat key terms consistently.
  Use the same terms, names or phrases when referring to main topics rather than mixing up synonyms.

- Project confidence.
  Use affirmative words and phrases to convey certainty and command of your material.
- Choose words with purpose.
  Every word choice either strengthens or weakens your presentation. Be intentional about language that educates, inspires and persuades audiences.

With mastery of language, presentations gain clarity, focus and eloquence. Audiences listen more attentively when content is expressed through thoughtful, precise wording. Whether you seek to inform, persuade or inspire, a speaker's linguistic choices shape the audience experience and amplify the overall impact of the message.

Practice

Quality practice is essential to maximize the effectiveness of your presentation. Investing time to rehearse thoroughly will help you refine content, smooth out any rough edges, and deliver with more polish and confidence.

Start by becoming extremely familiar with your material. Practice your presentation alone until you have it memorized as much as possible. This mastery of content will make your delivery smoother.

- Work on pacing.
  Time each section and your overall presentation during practice runs. If sections are too rushed or slow-paced, adjust to allocate time appropriately.
- Pay attention to transitions.
  Practice moving seamlessly from one point to the next using transition phrases like "Moving on" or "Turning to". Smooth transitions keep audiences oriented.
- Refine the conclusion.
  Many presentations end abruptly. Spend time perfecting a strong concluding statement that summarizes key points.
- Practice with visual aids and technology.
  Ensure you know how to smoothly operate slides, handouts, demos, or other elements you will use.

- Enlist others to watch a rehearsal.
  Ask for honest feedback on areas like pacing, gestures, and vocal variety. Incorporate their advice into the next practice round.
- Record your practice.
  Review the recording to see firsthand how your posture, expressions, tone and energy come across. Note improvements.
- Work on extemporaneous delivery.
  While you may rely initially on notes, shift to relying on bullet points and speaking extemporaneously to build flexibility.
- Pay attention to body language.
  Eliminate distracting mannerisms or gestures. Use movement purposefully to engage audiences.
- Refine your tone.
  Adjust volume, inflection, pauses and emphasis to highlight important ideas. A dynamic vocal delivery keeps attention.
- Simulate presentation conditions.
  Practice in a room setup similar to the actual presentation if possible, using any equipment you expect to have.
- Prepare for questions.
  Rehearse answers to possible questions that may arise. Think through how to respond on the fly.
- Relax with breathing exercises.
  Deep breaths before you present help manage nerves. Inhale slowly, pause, exhale fully. Repeat.

- Visualize success.
  Picture yourself presenting confidently and audiences responding positively. Mental imagery boosts confidence.

Proper practice makes presentations powerful. Taking time to prepare thoroughly helps control nerves, refine the delivery, smooth out rough edges, and ensure your presentation makes the impact you desire with audiences. The more you rehearse and hone the content, the more polished, authoritative, and compelling your presentation will be.

Chapter 3

Telling Stories and Using Humour

Audiences don't just want information, though that is often the main purpose of a speech or presentation. They also want to be entertained. The best wat to connect, communicate and convince is by using stories and humour.

People retain information better when they are in a receptive frame of mind, using relevant stories coupled with humour, will get your audience into that state of mind.

The following 6 points will help you determine which stories and what type of humour to use in order to better engage your audience.

1.   **Stories for Memorability**

      Stories make presentations more memorable. Narratives and anecdotes are easier for audiences to relate to and recall later.

2.   **Personal Stories**

      Personal stories build rapport. Brief stories from your own experience make you more relatable. Just keep them concise and relevant.

3.   **Know your audience**

Gauge whether stories and humour will resonate based on the audience culture and preferences. Adapt content accordingly.

4.   **Keep Stories Relevant**

Stories should make a point. Tie each story back to key themes and ideas in your presentation. Don't let stories become tangents.

5.   **Use of Humour**

Humour breaks down barriers. Laughter makes you more approachable and helps audiences relax. Use relevant, light-hearted humour sparingly to lighten the mood.

6.   **Keep Humour Natural**

Don't force humour. Humour should flow naturally from your style. Forced jokes and insincere laughter can undermine credibility.

Stories for memorability

Stories are a profoundly effective technique for making your key messages more memorable for audiences. Compelling stories engage listeners on an emotional level and create impactful mental images that are far easier to recall than bare facts or statistics alone.

Stories bring dry information to life. Presentation content full of data and bullet points can quickly bore audiences. A brief illustrative story woven throughout provides relief while also reinforcing your core ideas through examples. Stories enable you to showcase how concepts apply in the real world.

Narratives make messages tangible. Audiences may struggle to grasp intangible principles presented in the abstract. Telling a short anecdote featuring believable characters, vivid details and concrete actions ground your ideas in something relatable.

Stories appeal to emotions and imagination. Data triggers the rational left brain, while stories activate the right brain's visual cortex and emotional centres. This broader neurological activation cements memories.

Anecdotes create mental pictures. Humans remember in scenes and images. Even a brief scenario engages the imagination, painting a mental picture audiences can recall later.

Stories build connections. Hearing about experiences involving real people helps audiences relate to the material on a deeper human level. This empathetic bond boosts engagement.

Audiences put themselves in the story. When you introduce compelling characters and settings, listeners cannot help but envision themselves in that scene or role, heightening attention.

Narratives add variety. Lecturing audiences nonstop is fatiguing. Sprinkling in short stories provides a change of pace to reenergize them.

Stories make principles real. Abstract ideas come to life when framed as experiences lived by characters as opposed to theoretical concepts.

Anecdotes can simplify complex data. Highlighting one person's journey through detailed statistics makes the meaning more tangible.

Stories inspire and motivate. Hearing about others overcoming adversity often kindles audiences' own self-belief and determination.

The right stories make messages unforgettable. Audiences may not recall every fact in a presentation, but they will remember how the narrative made them feel and the insights it imparted. Stories give presentations heart and resonance.

Personal stories

Sharing brief stories and anecdotes from your own life can be a highly effective presentation technique. Personal stories make the speaker more relatable, add warmth, and lend authenticity to the messages being conveyed.

- Use personal stories sparingly.
  A few concise, well-chosen anecdotes spaced throughout the presentation will have more impact than long, rambling tangents.
- Keep stories focused.
  Only share experiences directly relevant to the core ideas of the presentation. Avoid meandering into unrelated topics.
- Have a clear takeaway.
  Any personal story should illustrate a key point or principle you want audiences to grasp. Tie the moral of your story back to your messages.
- Make it personal but not too private.
  Find the line between being transparent and oversharing inappropriately intimate details with professional audiences.
- Use self-deprecating humour.
  Poking fun at yourself displays vulnerability and makes you more approachable if done tastefully.
- Highlight challenges you've overcome.
  Describing difficulties you have pushed through shows perseverance and builds your credibility.

- Share your "origin story".
  Audiences love hearing the backstory of how you got started professionally or what led you here.
- Use the rule of 3.
  Set the scene, build up the challenge, then share the resolution. This satisfying arc sticks in memory.
- Use body language while telling stories.
  Maintain eye contact. Your posture and gestures should exude enthusiasm.
- Do not cover up nerves with rambling stories.
  Anxiety tempts some speakers to endlessly ad lib stories to avoid awkward silences.
- Practice transitions into and out of personal anecdotes.
  You want stories to flow naturally rather than feeling disjointed.
- Read the room.
  If audiences seem disengaged by extensive personal digressions, refocus the conversation on them.
- Solicit feedback afterward.
  Ask colleagues if they felt your stories were appropriate, relevant and added value.

With careful selection and delivery, brief personal stories forge powerful connections with audiences during a presentation. Used judiciously, they add warmth, empathy and vivid insights.

Know your audience

The stories you choose to incorporate into a presentation should directly reflect your audience and what is most relevant to them. Effective storytelling requires thoughtful understanding of who is listening and what anecdotes will best resonate with their interests, goals and pain points.

Know audience demographics. Are they predominantly Baby Boomers, Gen Xers, Millennials? The era someone grew up in may determine what cultural references they recognize.

Consider audience psychographics. What are their attitudes, values, beliefs? This influences what story themes align best. A tech-savvy crowd may appreciate different anecdotes than senior executives.

Understand the audience's knowledge level. You do not need to explain basic concepts or industry terminology in-depth to an expert crowd. But novices require more background setup.

Gauge the audience's desire for supporting evidence. Some accept anecdotes at face value while sceptical or data-driven listeners want statistics too.

Assess attention spans. Today's digitally distracted audiences may better absorb concise anecdotes rather than long, complex scenarios.

Be attentive to cultural diversity. Ensure language and examples are inclusive and avoid stereotypes. Consider translating key stories.

Know what resonates emotionally. What motivates this audience? Leadership principles? Social justice causes? Environmentalism? Look for stories aligned with their passions.

Reference familiar locales when possible. Audiences connect more with stories set in places they know rather than vague or foreign settings.

Understand company culture and goals. Industries have their own challenges. Tailor stories around issues the organization faces.

Observe audience reactions. If certain stories are met with blanks stares, switch approaches. Let their engagement guide you.

Ask audience members directly. Before presenting, interview a few about examples that influenced them personally.

Research audience interests. Scan industry publications, company websites and social media to gain insight on what captivates them.

While presentations often rely on data points and research to build credibility, strategically incorporated stories make the content more vivid, memorable and impactful for audiences. Know who is listening, what matters to them and what principles they value. Then shape your stories to resonate. Thoughtful audience understanding unlocks the full power of storytelling.

Keep stories relevant

When sharing stories in a presentation, remaining conscious of relevance is critical. Audiences will disengage if anecdotes seem tangential or drag on without a clear tie back to the core ideas. Follow these guidelines to keep stories tightly focused:

- Identify your objective.
  Before including a story, define specifically what point you want it to make. Don't add stories aimlessly.
- Limit set-up details.
  Avoid meandering background that bogs down the narrative. Jump quickly into the meat of the story.
- Watch story length.
  Stories should illustrate an idea concisely rather than dominating the presentation. Even compelling stories wear out their welcome.
- Link the takeaway.
  After finishing the story, explicitly state the lesson, principle or insight it conveyed relative to your message.
- Reinforce relevance.
  Remind audiences periodically how the story tied back to key themes if it was presented earlier in the talk.
- Omit unnecessary specifics.
  For example, the profession or hometown of characters likely doesn't need to be specified unless directly relevant.

- Exclude extraneous characters.
  Keep the focus on 1-3 central characters. Avoid diving into details around minor players not vital to the plot.
- Limit embellishment.
  Resist the temptation to over-dramatize or embellish details for dramatic flair. Keep it simple.
- Use callback humour sparingly.
  Brief callbacks are fine but don't overuse running gags to the point of distraction.
- Avoid stories for the sake of stories.
  Only include anecdotes strongly supporting your message, not just because they're entertaining tangents.
- Cut stories that aren't working.
  If you sense audiences losing interest during a story, it's okay to edit yourself and tie it off quickly rather than dragging it out.
- Keep characters relatable.
  Portray protagonists realistically. Perfect heroes that lack flaws may come across as unbelievable.
- Watch body language.
  If you see furrowed brows or audience members glancing at watches, wrap it up.

Always end stories clearly.

Tie the anecdote directly back to the core presentation takeaway before moving on.

With practice, you will develop an intuitive sense for when a story resonates or loses relevance. Audiences ultimately remember concepts more clearly when anchored by brief, focused stories rather than meandering narratives.

Use of humour

Used thoughtfully, humour can be a powerful presentation tool to captivate audiences and make messages more memorable. Laughter releases tension, fosters connections, and makes you more dynamic as a speaker. However, humour must be handled with care to avoid undermining your professionalism.

- Know your audience.
  Certain demographics or professions may find edgy humour inappropriate. Tailor jokes to align with audience sensibilities.
- Poke fun at yourself first.
  Self-deprecating humour displays confidence and makes you appear more relatable. Audiences enjoy seeing you not take yourself too seriously.
- Use relevant jokes and stories.
  Humour tightly integrated with your content shows you know the material inside and out. Avoid generic, canned jokes.
- Be self-aware.
  Understand your natural comedic strengths and weaknesses. Not everyone can deliver standup-quality material successfully.
- Limit impromptu humour.
  Occasional spontaneous quips can work well but avoid trying to be funny constantly off the cuff. Prepare humour ahead of time.

- Rein it in.
  A few well-placed jokes are enough. Trying to make the entire presentation humorous dilutes serious messages.
- Soften harsh news with humour.
  Difficult subjects go down easier with a bit of light-heartedness. But take care not to make light of serious issues.
- Smile and make eye contact when delivering a punchline.
  Your confidence and connection with the audience amplify the humour.
- Use callbacks sparingly.
  Brief references back to a previous laugh can work well but don't beat a joke to death through repetition.
- Highlight absurdities.
  Exposing silly contradictions in everyday life gently satirizes without putting others down directly.
- Stop trying if jokes are bombing.
  Don't harp on humour that isn't working. Quickly yet tactfully move on.
- Time delivery carefully.
  Ensure jokes do not sabotage the overall pacing. Audiences want to absorb content too, not just constant quips.
- Test humorous material.
  Try out jokes on trusted colleagues first to discern what works and what falls flat before going public.

- Leave profanity out.
  Swearing and vulgarity are regarded as crass,
  undermining your sophistication. Rely on cleverness
  instead.

Humour opens doors but it should never overtake substance.
When used carefully and considerately, funny stories and
light-hearted moments leaven presentations to hold
attention, stick in memories, and make audiences more
receptive to your ideas.

Keep humour natural

For humour to truly enhance a presentation, it must come across as organic and spontaneous rather than overly scripted or laboured. Attempting to insert jokes artificially frequently falls flat. Trust your natural comedic instincts and read the room to determine what resonates.

Do not try to be someone you're not. Let your distinctive personality and sense of humour shine through. Forced antics will look inauthentic.

Use humour naturally arising from content. Commenting spontaneously on amusing aspects of your material creates effortless laughs.

Relax and let go of the need to be funny. Taking yourself less seriously paradoxically makes humour emerge more freely.

Leverage your quirks. We all have harmless idiosyncrasies audiences find endearing. Highlight yours to add personalized charm.

Ad-lib occasional jokes inspired in the moment. Impromptu quips feel fresh compared to meticulously prepared gags, however resist going overboard.

Tell real stories from your life rather than fabricated yarns. Relatable tales from personal experience generate natural laughs.

Use self-deprecating humour with care. Poking fun at failures and foibles can work well yet avoid making yourself the butt of every joke.

React spontaneously to the environment. If something peculiar happens in the room, it's fine to point it out light-heartedly.

Watch for laughs you did not intend. when audiences chuckle unexpectedly, roll with it by acknowledging the humour. But steer the conversation back on track.

Smile, pause and make eye contact to emphasize laugh lines. Your delivery and connection amplifies the comedy.

Avoid over-explaining jokes that landed successfully. Nothing kills humour faster than belabouring the punchline. Move briskly onward.

Let awkward moments pass by. Attempting to force humour out of dead air typically exacerbates discomfort.

Limit distraction and disruption. Funny insertions should not upstage presentation flow.

Trust your instincts on appropriate boundaries. If a joke gives you pause, it may cross the line for audiences too. When in doubt, leave it out.

Ask trusted advisors for input on humour beforehand to gain perspective on how it will land in the room.

Audiences appreciate humour that emerges spontaneously from the speaker's personality. It creates space for audiences themselves to interject laughs too. When used judiciously, natural humour forges powerful connections. But forced comedy falls flat fast. Trust yourself and read the room.

Chapter 4

Using Body Language Effectively

The effective use of body language is exceptionally important when giving speeches and presentations. Standing at a lectern while gripping its sides and reading from your notes, might still get your message across. The audience will become bored quite quickly and drift off, perhaps missing some key points.

Using body language and stage movement will add power and interest to your presentation and keep the audience engaged longer. This gives you more time to Connect, Communicate and Convince.

The following 6 items will help you to use your body more effectively when giving speeches and presentations.

1. **Posture**
    Stand up straight with your shoulders back. This projects confidence and authority. Avoid slouching or leaning which can appear disengaged.

2. **Facial expressions**
    Use natural facial expressions to convey emotions fitting your content. Smile to appear warm and approachable. Let your face reflect passion or solemnity when appropriate. Avoid a flat, expressionless look.

3. **Gestures**

   Use purposeful hand gestures and movements. This adds dynamic visual interest. Motivated movements reinforce your message. Avoid distracting fidgeting or repetitive gestures.

4. **Movement**

   Move naturally around the stage if possible. Moving towards the audience invites engagement. Circling the stage adds energy. Avoid pacing nervously or standing stiffly in one spot.

5. **Energy**

   Project high energy and enthusiasm through your nonverbals. This captures audience attention and interest. Low energy appearing bored, tired, or uninterested tunes audiences out. Match your energy to your content.

6. **Eye contact**

   Make steady eye contact with your entire audience. This builds connection and interest. Don't stare anyone down or frequently look away.

Posture

Good posture is essential for effective public speaking. When giving presentations or speeches, how you hold and carry yourself impacts how audiences perceive you. Implementing proper postural techniques can help boost your delivery and connect with listeners.

Standing up straight with shoulders back and head high projects confidence and command. Slouching or leaning makes you appear unfocused and unprepared. Audiences read posture like body language – poor posture can undermine your authority, while good posture symbolizes control.

With good posture, you expand your lung capacity. Standing tall enables full, deep breaths. This allows sufficient breath support to avoid vocal strain. Proper breathing techniques prevent fatigue and vocal damage during long speeches.

When your posture is erect, your voice resonates optimally. Sound projects clearly outwards when your spine is vertically aligned. Slouching crunches the rib cage, restricting projection. Your voice cannot radiate out as freely, muffling articulation.

An upright stance also enables fluid gesture and movement. Shoulders back open the arms, freeing range of motion. You can use expansive, descriptive gestures without awkwardness. Moving around the stage appears natural, not encumbered.

Audiences view slouched, casual postures as sloppy and disengaged. This impression makes it harder to establish credibility and look polished. An attentive posture signals professionalism and care for the presentation.

With good posture, you also avoid nervous habits like slumping, swaying, or fidgeting. These distractions pull audience focus from the content. Proper postural alignment minimizes unintentional movements to keep eyes on you.

Specific postural tips for public speaking include:

- Stand with feet hip-width apart for balance. Avoid locking knees which can cause fainting.
- Align head over shoulders, not jutting forward. Chin should be vertical, not tucked down.
- Roll shoulders back and down, opening chest. Collar bones should spread, not hunch inward.
- Engage core muscles. Brace abdominals without holding breath. This supports the spine.
- Visualize a strong thread pulling from the crown of the head towards the ceiling. Elongate the neck.
- Distribute weight evenly between both feet. Do not favour one side. Keep knees soft, not rigidly locked.
- When gesturing, aim to return hands to neutral position near belly button or sides. Avoid fidgety hands.

With public speaking, first impressions matter greatly. Audiences begin assessing your authority and knowledge immediately. This makes those initial nonverbals incredibly impactful. Practicing proper postural alignment, even in rehearsals, trains your muscles to default to engaged, upright stances. This quickly becomes natural and comfortable. Good posture requires awareness and some effort initially, but pays dividends in boosting your delivery and audience connection.

Speakers who stand tall with confidence command attention, respect, and open minds.

Facial expressions

A speaker's face is centre stage, making facial expressions crucial during presentations. Audiences watch your face for nonverbal cues that reveal emotions and amplify your message. Mastering facial communication takes awareness and practice, but the payoff in audience engagement is immense.

Facial expressions act as visual punctuation to your speech. Raising eyebrows, smiling, frowning, and other movements help emphasize or react to content. Appropriate expressions educate audiences on how to interpret your words and feel about the implications.

For instance, pairing a serious or shocking statement with furrowed brows and a grim face underscores the gravity. Smiling while sharing a humorous anecdote tells audiences it's okay to laugh. Flashing an excited expression when announcing positive news generates shared enthusiasm.

Beyond punctuation, facial expressions foster connections with audiences. Presentations often feel formal and one-sided. Subtle facial expressions make you appear conversational and approachable. This perceived relationship makes audiences more receptive.

When speakers maintain a deadpan, expressionless face, audiences get bored and distracted. Without facial engagement, presentations risk seeming monotonous. Sparing, natural facial movements keep audiences focused by providing visual variety.

Yet expressions should not become exaggerated. Going overboard appears disingenuous or unintentionally comical. Subtlety is key. Here are tips for proper facial techniques:

- Let smiles develop slowly, not instantly flash on and off. This looks natural. Avoid smiling nonstop, which looks odd.
- Raise and furrow eyebrows in moderation. Infrequent movements are most impactful. Excessive wiggling seems cartoonish.
- Use eye contact to connect with different audience members. Avoid a wandering gaze. Make brief eye contact, not stare-downs.
- Allow some nervous mannerisms like brief lip-biting. This shows you're human. But avoid constant odd tics which can distract.
- Time facial expressions with verbal tone and gestures. All body language should coordinate to avoid mixed signals.
- Temper reactions based on audience and event formality. Be more subtle in professional contexts.
- If displaying sad expressions, finish with a reassuring, optimistic look to avoid leaving audiences downcast.
- Pause facial movement during audience reactions. Don't talk over laughter or applause. Smiling and nodding keeps you engaged without distracting.

A largely expressionless presentation risks seeming distant, indifferent, and robotic. Appropriate facial movement generates energy and forges bonds between speaker and listeners. Like gestures, posture, and vocal shifts, facial expressions turn static speeches into dynamic conversations. Savvy incorporation of facial techniques marks you as passionate, approachable, and genuinely excited to share your presentation.

Gestures

Gestures are vital visual tools for speakers. Hands lend expressiveness and dynamism to presentations, making them compelling to watch. Mastering strategic hand motions enhances descriptions, emphasizes points, and boosts audience engagement.

Gestures help paint mental pictures for audiences. Descriptions of size, shape, direction, and spatial relationships come alive through gestural representations. Hands can depict a small circle or wide rectangle, point left or right, and show nearness or distance. Simple gestures allow listeners to visualize concepts.

Strategic gestures also punctuate key points. Raising open palms outward on an important word spotlights its weight. Pointing to visual aids draws focus. Chopping one hand into the other underscores firmness or decisiveness. These motions help audiences recognize meaningful content.

Additionally, gestures make speakers appear conversational and comfortable. Reserved, static stances can seem stiff. Subtle hand motions give off vibrancy and confidence, engaging audiences. Movement generates energy and prevents monotonous delivery.

When using gestures:

- Keep them at waist level or above to stay visible. Avoid dropping hands too low.
- Use open palm gestures to demonstrate receptiveness. Fists or fingers can seem aggressive.

- Move hands in front of you or to the sides. Don't make distracting gestures behind or overhead.
- Avoid repetitive, distracting motions like jabbing or wringing hands.
- Gesture naturally with both hands, not just the dominant hand. Vary palm orientations.
- Time gestures to key words or phrases you want to accentuate. Don't gesture randomly.
- Let gestures flow from your centre core, not just forearms. This adds power to gestures.
- Return hands to neutral position near your side or front when not gesturing. Don't leave them dangling.
- Keep gestures visible by avoiding placing hands in pockets or behind a lectern.

With visual aids like slides, limit gestures to avoid competing. Refrain from pointing at screens constantly. Allow content to speak for itself.

Presenters who over-gesture or "flail" distract audiences. Nervous gesticulation also diminishes authority and conviction. But not gesturing at all makes delivery seem wooden. Strive for clear, concise, descriptive gestures at logical points.

When coordinated with posture, eye contact, and vocal pacing, strategic hand motions bring speeches to life. They lend colour and dynamism to words. Masterful gesturing boosts understanding of concepts, punctuates important content, and forges connections with audiences.

Movement

Movement is an influential yet often overlooked component of public speaking. How presenters utilize stage movement, walking patterns, and overall spatial awareness impacts audience engagement. When incorporated strategically, movement dynamics can profoundly enhance a speech.

Purposeful movement grabs audience attention. Our eyes naturally follow movement. Crossing the stage at key moments trains focus onto the speaker. This combats zoning out and distraction. Sudden moves or gestures also punctuate important content transitions.

Moving thoughtfully around the stage makes presentations more dynamic. Remaining bolted down in one spot grows monotonous, no matter how good the content. Changing spatial perspectives re-engages audiences and varies the visual landscape.

Movement allows audiences to see the speaker from all angles. Facing different directions ensures everyone gets direct eye contact and frontal views. This prevents a sense of exclusion or the speaker seeming to favour one section.

When presenting with visual aids, fluid movement between media prevents awkward dead air. Smoothly transitioning from screen to audience prevents a static, stilted experience. Changing positions seamlessly weaves together verbal and visual content.

Strategic movement tactics include:

- Crossing to the opposite side of the stage when making key new points. This physically embodies segues.
- Taking a couple slow steps towards the audience while making earnest appeals or dramatic statements. Eliminate barriers.
- Using space intentionally, not just aimless pacing. Each move should have purpose.
- Planting feet during important messages you want to sink in. Shifting weight also signals transitions.
- Not remaining behind lecterns or desks if avoidable. Break free of barriers.
- Moving naturally to your verbal rhythm and cadence. Accentuate phrases through movement.
- Looking at the audience while moving, not at the floor or notes. Maintain engagement.
- Avoiding distracting moves like repetitive circling or foot tapping.

Presenters should not force constant motion or choreography. Over-moving feels unnatural and distracting. The goal is strategic movement peppered in for dynamism and spatial connection.

With visual media, allow content time to breathe before moving again. Refrain from jumping around while the audience takes in slides or videos. Movement should enhance, not compete with, other content.

Overall, thoughtful movement makes presentations feel alive, not static. It grants spatial perspective to audiences while allowing speakers' personalities to shine through naturally. Movement manoeuvres audiences' eyes, bodies, and focus in sync with your content's flow.

Energy

A speaker's energy profoundly impacts audience engagement. High energy captivates listeners while low energy risks losing them. Strategically modulating energy level keeps audiences tuned in throughout a presentation.

Raising your energy introduces new sections and ideas. Boosting vocal variety, volume, pace, and passion when sharing key points signals their importance. High energy grabs attention, wakes up listeners, and drives concepts home.

You can also spike energy to punctuate messages you want to stick or stir emotions. Hammering forceful statements with zeal makes them impactful. Passionately pleading for audience participation inspires action. Energy underscores importance.

However, high energy should not be sustained constantly. While brief peaks of intensity engage, remaining at fever pitch eventually exhausts audiences. Fluctuating energy levels allows listeners to recover and refocus. Mixing high and low prevents fatigue.

Lowering energy provides balance and variety in tone. Casually conversational delivery during explanations gives audiences cognitive breaks. Pausing for laughs after jokes prevents trampling audience reactions. Solemnity in sombre sections comes through better with gravitas than fervour.

Strategic energy modulation tactics include:

- Raising volume, pace, and tension when sharing critical information to create focus.
- Boosting vocal power on key transition words like "however," "therefore," or "consequently" to stress relationships between ideas.
- Using passionate gestures and facial expressions to amplify emotional peaks. Energy should feel holistic.
- Projecting confidence during openings to command attention from the start. Strong introductions set the tone.
- Allowing pauses after impactful moments or visual reveals. This gives audiences time to absorb high-energy material.
- Speaking slowly and calmly when communicating complex data so listeners can comprehend details. Fast talking overwhelms.
- Reining in physical movements during serious or sombre sections. Low energy here feels appropriate.
- Monitoring audience energy and adapting accordingly. Boost your energy to recapture waning attention.

With the right balance, animated highs and relaxed lows carry audiences smoothly through pertinent peaks and valleys in a presentation's landscape. Avoid monotone monotony on one extreme and exhausting overzealousness on the other. An engaging ebb and flow of energy avoids distraction and fatigue while keeping listeners tuned in.

Eye contact

I have already written a section on eye contact in chapter 1 "Connecting with your audience". It is so important that I decided to write another section on it here.

Direct eye contact is a fundamental yet often overlooked public speaking skill. Proper eye contact techniques greatly enhance audience connection and engagement. By mastering eye contact, speakers appear poised, approachable, and conversational.

Fundamentally, consistent eye contact shows audiences they have the speaker's full attention. Speakers who stare at notes, screens, or the back wall appear distracted and indifferent. Frequent eye contact conveys respect, care, and focus on the message and listeners.

Eye contact also fosters individual connections, even in large crowds. Briefly looking directly at various audience members makes each feel personally addressed. This builds rapport crucial for receptiveness. People are far more responsive to speakers who make eye contact.

Beyond basic optics, eye contact indicates confidence. Speakers who maintain strong eye contact show poise and conviction in their material. Quickly glancing around or staring down reveals discomfort. Bold eye contact aligns with bold delivery.

When using eye contact effectively:

- Slowly scan the entire audience from left to right and front to back over time. Don't just fixate on one section. Change the pattern regularly to avoid looking robotic.
- Pause eye contact to glance briefly at visual aids, then return focus to the audience while discussing slides.
- Listen carefully to audience reactions like laughter or questions to determine where to direct eye contact.
- Following individuals with your gaze as they ask questions shows active listening and interest.
- Avoid zoning out by picking 3-4 audience spots to return your gaze to frequently. This keeps you anchored.
- Blink normally to avoid staring. Periodic breaks in eye contact alleviate intensity.
- Use eye contact to underscore important points. Locking in on the audience drives messages home.
- Be aware of cultural differences. Less direct eye contact may be appropriate in some settings. Gauge expectations.

Consistent eye contact takes practice for some, but rapidly improves with effort. It prevents disengagement, builds formidable audience bonds, and displays confidence and credibility. Speakers who immerse audiences in their gaze keep listeners transfixed and receptive.

Chapter 5

Mastering Your Voice and Tone

As with body language and stage movement having a monotone voice at the same volume for long periods will cause boredom in your audience and cause them to drift of and stop listening, they may well retain some information but if you really want to Connect, Communicate and Convince, adding richness and variability to your voice will make a massive difference.

The 6 points below will help you to keep your audience engaged throughout your speech or presentation.

1. **Enunciation**
    Clearly pronounce words and articulate consonants. Don't muffle or slur words. Precise enunciation improves comprehension.

2. **Resonance**
    Use diaphragmatic breathing to enhance resonance. Voice should come from the chest and mouth, not the nose. This amplifies and projects sound.

3. **Pacing**
    Vary speaking rate, slowing down for emphasis or speeding up to build excitement. Strategic pacing directs audience attention. Don't rush important points.

4. **Vocal Variety**
    Vary your volume, pitch, cadence, and inflection. This keeps your voice dynamic and engaging. Avoid monotone.

5. **Vocal Energy**
    Vary the power in your voice by using dramatic changes of volume and pace to emphasise key points in your message

6. **Pausing**
    Use strategic pauses to allow important points to sink in or highlight humour. Silence adds impact. Don't rush through nonstop.

Enunciation

Proper enunciation is vital for audience comprehension during speeches. Unclear, mumbled delivery risks losing listeners. By clearly pronouncing each word and syllable, speakers boost understanding of their message.

Enunciation focuses on articulating each sound in words fully and precisely. Every consonant and vowel should receive needed attention. This prevents "slurring together" words which obscures meanings. For instance, carefully pronouncing each syllable in "responsibility" avoids it becoming a muddled "responsi-bility".

Beyond enunciating, strategic pacing aids clarity. Trying to barrel through content too quickly garbles speech. Allowing judicious pauses between phrases gives audiences time to digest information. Attempting to rush through complex terms or concepts only bewilders.

For especially important points speakers want the audience to grasp, slowing rate of speech emphasizes clarity. Clearly pronouncing a critical word then briefly pausing before continuing underscores significance through tempo. This focused enunciation ensures comprehension.

However, speakers should avoid becoming too deliberate or over-enunciating constantly. This risks seeming patronizing or unnatural. The goal is clear, conversational speech, not a mechanically staccato delivery. Enunciation only needs spotlighting during moments of particular importance or complexity.

Tips for improving enunciation:

- Familiarize yourself thoroughly with any complex terms in your speech to avoid fumbling them. Practice problem words.
- If prone to speaking quickly when nervous, remember to consciously slow your rate in the moment.
- Use accurate descriptive gestures when saying key words. Gestures enhance enunciation's visual impact.
- Take deep breaths to keep air flowing smoothly. This powers clean vocal delivery.
- Break phrases into manageable chunks using pauses. This prevents mushing long sentences together.
- Record yourself practicing. Identify unclear passages needing better enunciation. Ask others what they had trouble understanding.
- If audiences frequently ask for clarification, focus on slowing and more precisely enunciating problem sections.

Remember, even the most fascinating speech content disappoints if audiences struggle to discern your words. Investing in clear, intelligible enunciation repays audiences with easy comprehension. You want listeners focused on your message, not decoding your delivery. Enunciation creates smooth vocal transmission of meaning and perspective.

Resonance

Resonance is the amplification and richness of vocal tone. Proper resonance allows a speaker's voice to fully carry throughout a space. Resonant voices grab attention and lend power to messages.

Resonance stems from optimal vocal fold vibration and strategic use of oral cavities. Voice originates in the larynx with vocal fold oscillation. This vibration produces sound waves that resonate in the pharynx, mouth, and nasal passages.

Proper posture assists resonance by opening the chest and throat. Slouching crunches the voice box, inhibiting full, free vibration. An upright stance aligns the throat and neck, creating space for resonance.

Poor resonance sounds thin, raspy, and limited in range. It fails to fill a room, requiring amplification. Resonant voices project clearly at appropriate volumes without strain. Sound resonates through open throat pathways.

Here are tips for improving vocal resonance:

- Hum or vocalize on an open "ah" vowel to feel resonance vibrating the roof of your mouth. Let sounds spin up and out.
- Focus tone forward in the mask of your face. Imagine sound spinning off the hard palate. Avoid nasal voices.
- Open your jaw to create more space. Clenching the jaw tightens throat muscles, constricting resonance.

- Picture your voice emanating from your sternum or forehead, not your throat. This lifts resonance.
- Smile slightly to lift your soft palate and create openness from mouth to nasal passages.
- Inhale through an open mouth, then exhale through your nose while vocalizing. This nasal buzz amplifies resonance.
- Avoid smoking, dehydration, and throat clearing which irritate and tighten vocal tissues.
- Do tongue trills, lip trills, and blowing raspberries to loosen up slack facial muscles and open your voice.

With an expanded vocal range and commanding projection, resonant voices seize listeners' attention. Words ring out effortlessly without strain. Resonance oils the vocal cords for peak performance in delivering speeches. After improving resonance, speakers sound more smooth, rich, and convincing. Their messages gain power and clarity.

Pacing

Proper pacing is essential for impactful public speaking. The pace or rate at which you speak conveys vital meaning beyond just words. Strategically varying pace, boosts audience engagement and punctuates content.

A moderate conversational pace works best for explanatory portions of a speech. Rapid-fire delivery overwhelms listeners struggling to absorb information. Overly slow speech risks boring audiences. A natural easy flow allows comprehension while maintaining interest.

However, occasional pace changes provide emphasis. Slowing way down when announcing critical data ensures the audience catches every detail. Quickening pace for excitement around successes builds momentum. These pace shifts orient audiences to significance.

Sudden dramatic pauses also punctuate content and spark curiosity. Pausing after a provocative question before answering prompts the audience to anticipate your response. Pacing variation creates cadence.

When using pacing effectively:

- Accelerate pace to convey urgency around pressing issues that demand action or awareness. Fast pace wakes audiences up.
- Slow way down if presenting complex concepts or unfamiliar terms. Allow audiences time to digest new information.

- Speed up narration of events slightly when recounting the exciting climax of a story. Faster pace mirrors rising action.
- Avoid habitually rushing through speeches. Nervousness causes quicker pacing but makes delivery unintelligible.
- Do not lapse into monotone plodding. This puts audiences to sleep. Even slow sections benefit from some energy.
- Remember that pauses permit powerful messages to sink in. Allow audiences a moment with significant ideas. Silence has purpose.
- Change pace mid-sentence at critical transition words like "however," "therefore," and "consequently" to stress relationships between ideas.

With experience, pace control becomes second nature. Ideally pace complements content rather than distracting from it. Fluid shifts in speed benefit novice and veteran speakers alike by showcasing vital information and reinforcing connections. Pacing brings speeches to life.

Vocal variety

Vocal variety is a crucial technique for captivating audiences during speeches. Variety in volume, tone, pitch, speed, and emphasis keeps delivery engaging. Monotone risks losing listener interest quickly.

Volume shifts grab attention and highlight important material. Briefly increasing volume emphasizes salient points. Quieter asides for humorous moments encourage audience participation. Whispering can draw listeners in during storytelling. Masterfully modulating volume signals meaning.

Varying tone also conveys meaning. A serious urgent tone stresses the gravity of issues. Light-hearted joyful tones uplift and motivate. Matching tone to content, from sombre to enthusiastic, helps connect with audiences.

Changing pitch breaks monotony. Altering where voice registers in your range makes ears perk up. Highlight key words using slightly higher pitches. Pitch changes introduce vocal texture and dynamics.

Pacing variation also captivates audiences. Quickening speed builds suspense. Slowing down underscores significance. Avoid constant pace which becomes a lulling metronome. Use pace for punctuation.

Emphasizing certain words through pauses, tones, and inflections points to nuances in meaning. Stress makes words punchy and memorable. Subtle shifts in emphasis work wonders.

Tips for employing vocal variety:

- Challenge yourself to shift volume, tone, pitch, or pace at least every sentence or two. Avoid prolonged monotony.
- Use dramatic pauses before announcing major news to capture suspense and attention. Two beats of silence builds anticipation.
- Insert humour or enthusiasm into your voice during lighter moments to give audiences permission to react and enjoy themselves.
- Stress words packed with meaning like powerful verbs by pausing slightly just before them. This spotlight grabs ears.
- Record yourself practicing and analyse when your voice becomes monotonous. Identify where shifts could heighten engagement.
- Note which techniques feel natural vs. forced. Allow variety to develop organically to avoid sounding disingenuous.

Keeping audiences actively listening for extended periods is challenging. Vocal variety acts like an unpredictable dance, keeping listeners on their toes. Purposeful shifts in delivery energize speeches and emphasize meaning in memorable ways. With vocal variety, words leap off the page into vivid life.

Vocal energy

Vocal energy is a speaker's power, enthusiasm and vocal dynamics. High vocal energy electrifies audiences while low energy bores. Strategically modulating vocal energy over a speech's course maximizes impact.

Bursts of passionate vocal energy introduce new ideas. Sharing key points loudly, forcefully or joyfully signals their importance. Ramped up volume, power and intensity grab ears and minds. High energy sections should activate audiences.

However, vocal energy requires thoughtful ebb and flow. Prolonged intense shouting exhausts audiences. Starting quietly after high energy moments also effectively contrasts dynamism. Vocal energy fluctuations allow necessary rests between animations.

Lowering energy provides balance against intensity. A conversational tone for explanations gives audiences needed cognitive breaks. Low energy sections should avoid monotony but feel measured. Gravity or solemnity carry through better with controlled calm than continual fervour.

Tips for effectively managing vocal energy:

- Raise volume and quicken pace when sharing critical information to capture attention. Punch key words.
- Drive home important ideas by slamming verbal punctuation, like hitting consonants crisply. Bold delivery boosts retention.

- Get creative with vocal sound effects. Things like dramatic whispers and gasps punctuate speech at poignant moments.
- Avoid monotone droning by injecting flavour and passion into your voice. Even during slower portions, use inflection.
- Speak slowly and steadily when communicating complex data so audiences can fully digest details. Fast talking overwhelms.
- Watch audience energy and adapt yours accordingly. Increase dynamics to pump up low energy crowds.

With experience, vocal energy modulation becomes second nature. The ideal balance energizes audiences without tiring them. Fluctuating between bold, striking delivery and calmly conversational explanation keeps listeners tuned in. Vocal energy dynamism makes speeches come alive.

Pausing

While words convey surface-level meaning during speeches, strategic silences speak volumes. Effective use of pauses profoundly punctuates content, allowing messages to sink in deeply. Mastering the pause elevates public speaking.

Pauses highlight important ideas. Pausing after sharing a vital statistic or concept gives the audience a moment to absorb it. This active silence signals gravitas and promotes retention. Rushing on deprives listeners of time to process significance. A few beats of silence linger meaningfully.

Dramatic pauses also build suspense and interest before revealing key points. Drawing out silence before announcing critical news, prompts audience anticipation. When deployed before a punchline, pauses prime the audience for laughter. Suspense and relief keep attention locked in.

Additionally, pauses prevent speaker overload. Allowing breathing room at natural syntax points gives the audience cognitive breaks between dense chunks of content. This promotes comprehension and retention. Nonstop rapid-fire delivery tends to sail past listeners.

To harness the power of silence:

- Resist the urge to rush through prepared remarks and instead allow thoughtful pauses. This creates cadence, not constant noise.
- After asking the audience a question, pause a few seconds before answering yourself. This gives them a chance to actively respond.

- Avoid speaking over audience reactions like laughter or applause. Pause to acknowledge responses before continuing.
- If feeling nervous is causing a tendency to speed talk, remind yourself to slow down and incorporate more pauses for effect.
- To avoid awkwardly long pauses, mentally count one or two beats before proceeding. This provides fluid pacing.
- Listen carefully to gauge when audiences need moments of silence to fully respond to content before continuing vocally.

Learning to step back and yield the stage through silent pauses counterintuitively amplifies the power of words. Noise can blur together into forgettable monotony. Consciously incorporating pauses adds colour, suspense, weight, and moments to breathe. Mastering silence transforms speeches into engaging conversations.

Chapter 6

Using Visual Aids to Enhance Your Presentation

Using Visual aids is a great way to grab your audience's attention. They will add interest but should be used to complement your message and not just because they look good. Many slide decks are boring and text heavy. This will cause your audience to read ahead and stop listening to you, making it extremely difficult to Connect, Communicate and Convince.

The following 6 tips are all about using slides, but don't forget you can use physical props as well.

1. **Keep visuals simple**
    Use minimal text and clean, uncluttered designs. Avoid crowded slides. Let the images tell the story.

2. **Use high-quality visuals**
    Make sure any photos or graphics you use are high resolution. Pixelated or distorted images will detract from your presentation.

3. **Use colour strategically**
    Colours can evoke emotions and emphasize key points. But don't go overboard. Stick to 2-3 colours and make sure there is enough contrast between text and background.

4. **Use charts and graphs to illustrate data**
   Visual representations of statistics and trends are often easier for audiences to grasp than numbers alone.

5. **Animate with purpose**
   Subtle animations can help convey information but avoid excessive or distracting transitions. Let animations highlight important points.

6. **Limit text**
   Slides should complement you, not substitute you. Use bullet points instead of full sentences. Keep text short, large, and easy to read.

Keep visuals simple

When creating visual aids for a presentation or speech, it's important to keep the design simple and streamlined. Avoiding clutter and distraction will allow your visuals to better support your message. A clean, straightforward visual communicates more effectively than one that is dense with excessive text, complex data, or confusing charts and graphs.

Follow the rule of less is more. You want your visuals to reinforce what you are saying, not compete with you for the audience's attention. Remove any elements that do not directly contribute to the core point you are trying to make with that slide. For example, don't include a company logo or branding on every slide unless it serves a purpose. Ask yourself if every word, image, shape, and colour on the slide enhances the message or creates unnecessary distraction.

When deciding how much information to include on a slide, limit text to key phrases, main ideas, and short bullet points that highlight your talking points. You do not want slides to just display dense paragraphs that attendees could simply read themselves. Avoid cramming slides with numbers, statistics, and facts. Pare down data to only the most relevant and impactful points that will resonate with the audience.

For text, choose a simple, clean font that is large enough to read from the back of the room. Font styles that are too elaborate or ornate can distract. Text should have high contrast from the background colour. Dark fonts on light backgrounds work better than light fonts on dark.

Consistent use of the same font throughout all visuals creates a unified, professional look.

Images should relate directly to the topic and not be overly complicated. Simple bar and pie charts are easier to quickly comprehend than intricate infographics. Pictures should clearly illustrate an idea, not just decorate. When selecting photographs, make sure they are high quality and not pixelated, distorted, or fuzzy when projected at a larger size.

Minimal use of colour is best for backgrounds and text. Stick to one or two colours that align with your brand and look professional. Avoid wild, neon colours that fatigue the eyes. A basic white or grey background is clean and neutral. Blue is an excellent text colour for conveying trust and confidence.

Animations like builds, transitions, and movement should also be simple and subtle. Avoid anything too flashy or gimmicky. The focus should be on the presenter, not the slides. Movement should smoothly transition between ideas, not distractingly appear on the screen.

Following the principle of simplicity will ensure your presentation visuals amplify your speech rather than compete with it. Slides are meant to be visual support for the presenter, not act as cue cards or prompts. By keeping slides clean, clear, and concise, you allow the audience to better connect with your core message.

Use high-quality visuals

Using high-quality visuals in your presentations and speeches is critical for maintaining a professional, polished look that engages your audience. With today's high-resolution projectors and screens, any flaw in your visuals will be glaringly obvious to the audience. Avoid amateurish, pixelated images by taking time to select and create visuals that enhance your talk.

For images, always obtain high-resolution versions that will not become distorted or degraded when projected. Avoid basic clipart or heavily compressed JPGs that will look obviously blurry and pixelated when enlarged on a big screen. Seek out images that are at least 1080p or higher resolution. If selecting photographs, make sure they are shot with quality equipment and are crisp when zoomed in. Also ensure your image files are a reasonable file size - not too low resolution to be blocky but not so massive they slow down your presentation.

When creating your own charts and graphs in PowerPoint, export them as PNG or vector files rather than JPG to maintain quality. Make sure charts and data visualizations are clear, legible, and convey information easily to the audience. Avoid overcomplicating data that looks busy on a slide.

If using text over images, ensure the text stands out clearly and is not obscured by busy backgrounds. Apply solid fills or contrasts to help text pop. Avoid light fonts on light backgrounds or dark on dark. Make sure to use high-resolution logos that will not become pixelated or distorted.

Where possible review your visuals on the same presentation setup and equipment you will use for the actual talk. Image quality can vary hugely on different screens. You want to be sure colours, clarity, text size, and overall quality look professional. If some visuals look subpar on the projector, go back and adjust so nothing appears amateurish when presented.

Proof your slides to fix any pixelation, fuzzy images, jaggies, compression artifacts, colour banding, or other issues that detract from quality. Zoom in and inspect at 100% to check for problems. Fix overly small text that will be difficult to read. Review your exported slides to catch any loss of quality from the original files.

Credit all stock photos and images appropriately with sources. Make sure you have rights to use any visuals in your presentation to avoid legal issues.

Offer high-quality handouts, if relevant, so audience members have a useful takeaway. Use sufficiently thick paper and high-resolution colour printers. Slides with tiny text do not translate well to standard black-and-white photocopied handouts.

With ample time and attention to detail, you can ensure your presentation looks polished, crisp, and professional. Audience members will recognize high-quality visuals that reinforce your expertise and credibility. Investing in well-designed visuals makes an impression and elevates your public speaking.

Use colour strategically

Strategic use of colour in your presentation and speech visuals helps convey key messages, direct focus, and keep visuals aesthetically pleasing. Colour evokes emotions and meanings that can subtly influence your audience when used effectively.

Limit your colour palette to two or three colours maximum. Monochromatic colour schemes with shades of one colour are calm and soothing. Complementary colours like blue and orange are vibrant when used together. Avoid overusing brightly discordant colours that fatigue the eyes.

Establish a colour scheme early and use it consistently across all presentation slides. This creates a cohesive, unified aesthetic. Vary shades of your chosen colours for visually stimulating variety.

Be mindful of colour associations. Blue conveys trust, red communicates urgency, green signifies growth. Use colours to align with your brand identity or reinforce themes. For example, green on slides about sustainability.

Ensure all text has high contrast with background colours. Dark text on light backgrounds offers the best contrast. Light text on dark backgrounds reduces legibility. Check that coloured text does not visually vibrate against the background.

Use bold, bright colours to highlight important text, headings, and key points. This draws the audience's attention. Softer muted colours recede into the background. Use strategically to direct focus.

Colour-code concepts, data, and categories across your presentation for clarity. For example, always visualize Category A in blue and Category B in red. Consistent color-coding aids comprehension.

In charts and graphs, limit data to two or three coloured lines or bars for easy differentiation. Any more colours become difficult to decipher. Pick visually distinct colours like blue, orange, and green rather than similar hues.

Avoid overly flashy animations and transitions in loud neon colours that feel unprofessional. Subtle builds and transitions in muted tones integrate smoothly without distracting.

Be aware some colours like red and green are difficult for colour-blind viewers to distinguish. Choose colour-blind friendly palettes if relevant or include patterns with colours to differentiate.

Ensure your colours project well on the presentation setup and do not look washed out or pixelated. Some hues translate better than others under bright lights. Have backup colour options if needed.

Printed handouts should use black and white friendly colour schemes, or you must print colour handouts. Coloured text and elements may become illegible when converted to grayscale.

Carefully check for and fix any unintended coloured artifacts, line remnants, or inconsistent use of colour across slides. Consistency with colours is key for a polished look.

With strategic use of colour, you can visually convey key information, set the right tone, and make your visuals more aesthetically powerful. Colour should always enhance your presentation rather than distract the audience. A few well-chosen colours go a long way in engaging viewers.

Use charts and graphs to illustrate data

Using well-designed charts and graphs to visualize data can make your presentations more impactful and easier for audiences to comprehend. Displaying data visually enhances retention and allows viewers to grasp complex concepts efficiently.

When presenting statistics and figures, converting raw numbers into graphical visuals simplifies and clarifies the data for audiences. For example, plotting survey results on a pie chart rather than showing a table of percentages.

Carefully select chart types that best illustrate the data insights you want to focus on. Bar charts easily compare quantities. Line charts show trends and changes over time. Pie charts showcase proportional breakdowns. Scatter plots visualize correlations. Pick appropriate, meaningful visualizations.

Keep chart designs and palettes simple, clean, and consistent across your presentation. Overly ornate or haphazard visual styles confuse viewers. Maintain a unified aesthetic using minimalist designs, limited colour schemes, clean fonts, and clear labels.

Ensure text is large enough to be readable for audience members. Use brief, descriptive labels and legends. Omit unnecessary words and numeric precision that clutter the visuals. Round numbers for easier comprehension.

Only include relevant data. Do not overwhelm the audience with too many data points plotted simultaneously. Focus each chart on illustrating one key takeaway or finding.

Use visual cues like arrows, callouts, or colour coding to highlight notable data points you wish to emphasize in your speech. Guide the audience's eyes.

Explain the significance of the data displayed and provide context. Do not assume audiences will inherently make the connections you wish them to see. Explicitly state key insights.

Only animate minimal chart elements to maintain attention on you as the speaker, not the visuals. For example, you may build selected data bars incrementally but avoid unnecessary flashy motion.

Test charts and graphs on the presentation setup. Ensure colours, text, lines, and data markers will be clearly visible from the back of the room when projected. Account for visibility and legibility issues.

Use high resolution images for crisper visuals. Pixelated, fuzzy, or compressed charts undermine professionalism. Recreate any graphs in presentation software rather than screenshots if needed.

Cite external data sources appropriately on slides. Only present accurate, unaltered data to maintain credibility. Do not misconstrue figures to fit narratives.

With strategic use of meaningful charts and graphs, you can make data more accessible, memorable, and impactful for your audience. Visualizing key data insights elevates a presentation.

Animate with purpose

When used thoughtfully, subtle animations in your presentation visuals can elegantly emphasize key points and transition between ideas smoothly. However, overdoing flashy animations can feel gimmicky and distract from your speech. Animation should enhance your content, not compete with it.

First, limit animations like builds, transitions, and motion to only what enhances your narrative or draws attention to important concepts. Avoid animating everything on your slides just because you can. Restraint with animations conveys professionalism and focuses the presentation.

For text, limit animations to the main headings, key takeaways, or critical data you wish to emphasize in sequence. For example, you may fade in three key bullet points one by one as you discuss each. Avoid having entire paragraphs of text fly in word-by-word, which feels disjointed.

When graphically displaying data comparisons, use subtle build animations to introduce data series incrementally. For instance, you might have sales figures for different regions appear on a bar chart one set at a time while discussing the regional differences. This progression directs the audience's focus in sync with your narrative.

Animations can also smoothly transition between ideas on different slides with continuity. For example, having a pie chart seamlessly morph into a new bar chart maintains forward momentum. But avoid transitions that feel chaotic or jarring.

Choose animation designs that aesthetically fit your overall presentation look. Maintain a style cohesive with fonts, colour schemes, and layouts on your slides. Over-the-top animations that seem disjointed from your visual brand simply distract rather than enhance.

Beware of excessive slide transition animations between every slide that become tedious. Use sparingly and consistently when transitioning between major topics or sections. Fancy transitions should not distract from the core content.

Test animation timing along with your presentation flow. Make sure pacing of animations aligns smoothly with your verbal guidance, neither lagging nor jumping ahead of your speech. Refine timing as needed.

Do not rely on animations to cue you through the presentation. As the speaker, you should drive the flow, not the visuals. Animations should support your narrative, not lead it.

Check that motion allows enough time for viewers to fully process information before moving ahead. Fast, frenetic animations can become difficult to comprehend. Build in strategic pauses.

Overall, approach animations with intentionality and purpose. Seamless, subtle motion that enhances key data points, transitions, and narrative flow will elevate your presentations when used strategically. But overly flashy, excessive animations detract rather than amplify. Animation should complement you as the speaker, not compete as the main event.

Limit text

In presentation slides, text should be used minimally and purposefully. Your slides are meant to complement you as the speaker, not serve as prompts or become a script to be read. By limiting text, you keep the audience's attention focused on your words.

Follow the 6x6 rule - no more than 6 words per line and 6 lines per slide. This prevents dense blocks of text that are difficult to read and disengage audiences. Use concise phrases, key terms, and short bullet points rather than full sentences or paragraphs. Treat this is a maximum and not a target. Less is better.

Text should reinforce what you are saying verbally, not duplicate it. Avoid spelling out details the audience can simply read themselves. Slides are meant to visualize your points, not act as handouts. Reduce explanations, descriptions, and definitions to key essentials only.

Font size should be large enough to easily read from the back of the room - generally at least 24 point for slide titles and 18 point for body text. Avoid tiny font sizes that strain the audience's eyes.

Limit text to 2-3 simple, clear points per slide to avoid overloading viewers. Break complex topics down into multiple slides rather than cramming all information into one dense visual.

Only include text that is truly necessary and relevant to your speech. If words do not amplify your verbal message in some way, remove them. Adhere to clear, concise phrasing.

Use consistent fonts, sizes, colours, and styles across all presentation slides. This unity projects professionalism and aids readability. Avoid cluttered slides with multiple conflicting text designs.

Left align text rather than full justifying, which creates uneven word spacing. Left aligned text with clean line breaks maximizes readability.

Use text colours with strong contrast against the slide background to maximize legibility for the audience. Light text on dark backgrounds reduces readability.

Proofread slides to fix errors that both distract and undermine your credibility as a professional presenter. Typos are glaringly obvious on a large projected screen.

Animating text onto slides word-by-word or line-by-line is tedious for audiences and can quickly become a distraction. Reveal text all at once in key moments instead.

Never read full paragraphs or sentences directly off slides. Refer to slides to reinforce key points, not provide a word-for-word script. Maintain eye contact with the audience as much as possible.

In summary, limiting how much text appears on each slide, while also maximizing its formatting for clarity and legibility, allows your slides to effectively support your speech rather than pull attention away from you as the speaker.

Follow the "less is more" principle with text to amplify your presentation.

Know your material. Go through your presentation outline and make sure you understand the flow and key points. Memorize any facts, statistics, or quotes you plan to include.

Chapter 7

Practicing and Rehearsing Your Presentation

Quality practice is one of the key factors to successful speeches and presentations. Remember its practice not rehearsal. We don't need to, or even desire to, be word perfect. We need to know our material and how it should flow, but still leave room for spontaneous use of language to keep our presentations looking and sounding fresh. To Connect, Communicate and Convince, we need to keep our audience's attention.

Following the next 6 tips will ensure that our practice helps keep people engaged throughout.

1. **Know your content**
    Know your content thoroughly. Go through your presentation outline multiple times until you have a deep understanding of the flow, key points, and details. This will make you feel more confident when presenting.

2. **Practice out loud**
    Practice out loud and with slides/visuals. Verbalize your presentation from start to finish, using your slides or visual aids. Get comfortable transitioning between slides and talking through the content.

3. **Practice with equipment**
   Practice with equipment and, where possible in the presentation space. Get familiar with the projection, mic, pointer remote, etc. Walk through the physical space to optimize movement and flow.

4. **Record yourself**
   Record yourself. Use your phone or computer to record video or audio as you rehearse. Play it back to see where you can improve your delivery.

5. **Get feedback**
   Ask a trusted friend or colleague to watch your practice run. Have them point out where you appear awkward or uncertain. Thank them for their honesty.

6. **Visualize success.**
   Picture yourself presenting smoothly, confidently, and effectively. Imagine the audience reacting positively. Mental imagery can boost self-assurance.

Know your content

Knowing your content is one of the most important aspects of giving an effective presentation or speech. When you thoroughly understand the material you are presenting, you will speak with greater confidence, authority, and passion. Audiences can sense when a speaker is not fully prepared, and it will undermine your credibility. Here are some key reasons why knowing your content inside and out is so critical for public speaking success:

- Preparation builds confidence.
  When you have taken the time to deeply research and comprehend your topic, you will feel far more self-assured when it is time to present. You won't be consumed with worries about whether you know the information well enough or if you'll draw a blank. That peace of mind allows you to focus fully on your delivery and connecting with the audience. Even experienced speakers feel nervous before big presentations, but preparation is what steadies those nerves.
- You can speak conversationally.
  Knowing your content means you do not have to robotically read verbatim off a script or slides. You can riff, use storytelling techniques, and speak conversationally. This engages audiences far more effectively than a stiff, over-rehearsed delivery. When you are free to make eye contact and "speak from the heart," audiences are much more likely to listen attentively and retain information.

- You can emphasize key points.
  When you have a mastery of the content, you will intuitively know how to stress the most important elements. You will be able to read the room and re-focus the presentation if the audience seems confused or disengaged. Audiences appreciate when speakers highlight takeaways and repeat crucial information using different analogies and examples. This type of reinforcement sticks with listeners long after the presentation ends.

- It allows for storytelling.
  Mastering the content means you can properly incorporate storytelling techniques that capture audience attention. Stories make presentations memorable, relatable, and impactful. But you must know the key data points well enough to weave narratives around them naturally. Stories lose power if it seems like the speaker is straining to remember facts and figures while telling them.

- You avoid errors.
  There is little more embarrassing when speaking than making an obvious factual error because you failed to properly learn the content. Not only does it damage your credibility, but you may have to waste valuable time backtracking and correcting yourself. That ends up muddling the message and confusing listeners. Thorough preparation is the best way to mitigate this risk.

- You can read nonverbal cues.
  When you are not glued to your notes, you can make eye contact and "read the room" to gauge how the audience is responding. You will notice if people look puzzled and know when you need to slow down, clarify, or re-approach a topic. Reading nonverbal signals allows you to adapt your delivery and ensure understanding. This is only possible if you have the content locked in.

- It makes listening easier.
  Audience members must mentally process a great deal of information during a presentation. This effort is reduced if the speaker clearly knows the material and delivers it competently. Learning is easier when audiences are not distracted by a speaker who seems out of their depth or disorganized. Knowing your stuff helps listeners comprehend and retain.

- You appear authoritative.
  Audiences want to have faith in speakers as trusted experts. Knowing the subject matter backwards and forwards is what earns that authority. When it is clear you have "done your homework," audiences will have far more respect for your opinions and conclusions. Nothing diminishes credibility faster than a presenter who does not command their content. Preparation establishes that command.

In summary, knowing your material thoroughly is a prerequisite for impactful public speaking. It builds confidence, allows for an engaging delivery, reinforces key points, handles questions, enables storytelling, avoids errors, reads nonverbal cues, aids listening, creates authority, and shows respect for audiences. Great presenters know there are simply no shortcuts - they must master the content first. This earns the trust of audiences. Preparation provides freedom. The more you know, the more comfortably and powerfully you can present.

Practice out loud

Simply knowing your material is not enough when it comes to delivering an impactful speech. You must also practice presenting out loud. This serves several key purposes:

- It builds vocal power.
  Your voice is your most important tool as a presenter. Practicing out loud develops proper breath support to project clearly without straining. It also varies tone and inflection, so you sound dynamic not robotic. Physical rehearsal helps eliminate distracting filler words like "um" and "ah" as well. Mastering voice mechanics is vital.

- It improves pacing.
  Speaking aloud allows you to pace yourself correctly so the delivery feels natural, not rushed. You learn where to pause for emphasis or transitions between key points. Proper pacing ensures you stay within time limits and keeps audiences engaged. It is harder for minds to wander when the speaker has good rhythm and cadence.

- It boosts memorization.
  Repeating the speech out loud taps into verbal memory and helps you internalize the content. This allows for smoother storytelling and eye contact when it is time to present. You will be relying less on slides or notes to remember what comes next. Memorization takes repetition, and vocal practice reinforces memory.

- It enhances body language.
  Good presentations are not just about words. Practicing in front of a camera helps you develop effective gestures and facial expressions. Things like hand movements, smiles, and eye contact will come across more naturally with rehearsal. Avoid distracting mannerisms and use your body to convey confidence.
- It allows for refinement.
  Initially, your speech may be too complex, dry, or long. Rehearsing out loud allows you to identify where it drags, where humour falls flat, where a story meanders, or where more explanation is needed. Practice leads to polish. Refinements come from hearing your own speech versus just reading silently on paper.
- It builds confidence.
  Confidence comes from competence, and nothing breeds competence like practice. Hearing yourself present smoothly in rehearsal gives a mental assurance boost before the big day. You will know precisely what to expect because you have already been through it multiple times. This relieves stress and anxiety.
- It highlights problem areas.
  When practicing out loud, you may fumble over certain complex passages or feel like you are rushing at certain transition points. Out loud rehearsal pinpoints these issues so they can be addressed. If you only rehearse internally, you will miss these performance problems until you are live.

- It allows for audience feedback.
  Practice your speech in front of colleagues, friends or family. Their reactions will show where content is confusing, stories drag or volume needs adjusting. They can also gauge whether the speech meets time limits. Audiences provide insight you cannot get rehearsing alone.
- It ensures proper understanding.
  It is common to think you know your speech content because you wrote it. But saying it aloud may reveal gaps in understanding you did not recognize reading silently. Practicing orally deepens comprehension and cements the speech in memory. Do not assume you know it until rehearsed out loud.
- It reduces dependence on notes.
  With proper run-throughs, you will rely less on detailed notes or slides. This allows for more eye contact and dynamic delivery. Nothing diminishes audience connection faster than a presenter buried in their notes. Practicing imprints the content so your eyes can stay on the crowd.

In summary, out loud practice is essential for impactful speeches. It hones voice mechanics, improves pacing, boosts memorization, develops physical stamina, enhances body language, allows refinement, builds confidence, highlights problem areas, garners feedback, ensures comprehension, reduces dependence on notes and builds vocal endurance. Great presentations require meticulous rehearsal. Knowledge and preparation lead to powerful delivery. Practicing out loud is a speaker's best insurance policy for success.

Practice with equipment

In addition to knowing your content and vocal rehearsal, it is critical to practice, where possible, using the actual equipment you will have in place during the presentation. Failing to do this can trip up even the most prepared speakers. Practicing with the full setup achieves several objectives:

- It prevents technical glitches.
  Microphones, projectors, clickers and other equipment often have quirks or need proper setup. Rehearsing ensures sound levels are right, slides advance smoothly, and connections work. You can confirm batteries are charged and positions are adjusted. Troubleshoot problems now, not when live.
- It allows slide timing.
  Run through the speech with the visuals to perfect slide changes and pacing. Ensure content matches with imagery and builds at the right speed. Slides that feel too quick or slow can be fixed when rehearsed in full. Do not wing this timing; it is too important.
- It builds physical familiarity.
  Get a feel for the stage, lectern, chairs and lighting so the environment is familiar. Make sure you can move freely and access slides or notes. Know if cord length limits mobility. This reduces stress versus entering the room cold on speech day. Rehearse in similar clothing too.

- It reinforces memorization.
  Standing at the lectern using your real notes, or walking the stage, reinforces memory far better than sitting at a desk. The more lifelike the rehearsal, the stronger your recall will be under pressure. Use this mental encoding time to cement the flow in your mind.
- It boosts confidence with equipment.
  Unfamiliarity breeds anxiety and uncertainty. Practicing on site with the full setup – microphone, clicker, computer, lights, etc. – makes it feel known and routine. Being at ease with the equipment projects confidence to audiences.
- It allows for sound adjustments.
  Determine if you need to speak louder, closer to the mic or change levels to suit the room acoustics. Offsite practice does not account for room size and echo. Make amplification adjustments based on the real location.
- It tests sightline issues.
  Make sure audiences in the back rows can see screens and presentation materials. Adjust fonts, graphics, pointer lasers if visuals are unclear from afar. Only onsite practice reveals these distance problems.
- It allows room familiarity.
  Learn where audience members will sit, entrances, exits and any potential distractions like outside noise or food service. Make a mental note of these so you remain focused. You want no surprises on event day.

- It tests lighting options.
  Make sure projection screens are visible with normal lighting. Adjust glaring or dim lights as needed. Lighting often looks different before an audience arrives. Make sure you can easily see notes and computer screens.
- It allows recording.
  Record a rehearsal to critique yourself later. Watch for distracting mannerisms, pacing issues, etc. Reviewing your rehearsal video avoids being overly self-critical listening live. This provides an objective eye.
- It gives time to edit.
  Onsite practice may reveal the need to adjust volume, fonts, colours or trim content if running long. Rehearse enough in advance to allow edits. Do not put this off until the last minute.

In summary, practicing on location with the full technical setup is invaluable. It avoids technical glitches, perfects slide timing, builds familiarity, reinforces memorization, boosts equipment confidence, adjusts sound, tests sightlines, allows room familiarity, checks lighting, enables videotaping and provides time to edit. Treat the rehearsal space like showtime. The more realistic, the better. This minimizes surprises and instils the confidence and muscle memory needed for powerful delivery when it truly counts.

Record yourself

In addition to rehearsing out loud and with equipment, recording your practice speeches is incredibly helpful. Both video and audio recordings provide valuable feedback you cannot get while presenting live. Here are some key benefits:

- It shows presentation flaws.
  It is easy for speakers to miss poor body language, distracting mannerisms, excessive ums and ahs, pacing issues, etc. while caught up in practice. Recordings reveal these problems objectively. You may wince at moments, but you can correct them.
- It allows nonverbal analysis.
  Watch your facial expressions, posture, gestures, and movement. Make sure they convey confidence and enthusiasm. Look for nervous tics like playing with hair or swaying. Keep hands low and limiting fidgeting. Let positive nonverbals reinforce your message.
- It enables vocal critique.
  Listen to volume, tone, quality and cadence. Is your voice dynamic or flat and lifeless? Do you enunciate and avoid vocal fillers? Are there excessive pauses or awkward phrasing? Pinpoint vocal imperfections to strengthen.

- It highlights content issues.
  Review recordings to make sure information flows logically, stories transition smoothly, humour lands properly, and explanations are clear. Edit anything that seems disorganized or confusing. Repetition in different contexts cements ideas.
- It reinforces memorization.
  Do sections from memory during recording to simulate delivering without notes. This mental rehearsal imprints the speech even deeper. Review recordings to identify areas that still need reinforcement.
- It gauges time limits.
  Time your recorded practice runs so you learn your speech duration. This allows time for proper editing so content fits allotted slots. Nerves tend to speed up delivery, so build in extra cushion.
- It boosts confidence.
  Seeing and hearing yourself present smoothly in rehearsal builds assurance and familiarity. You will know what to expect on speech day. Review tapes to remind yourself of areas done well too!
- It allows peer feedback.
  Ask colleagues or friends to watch and critique your recorded practice. They can offer insights you may miss watching alone. Welcome constructive feedback to perfect the presentation.

- It enables self-critique.
  It is easy to judge ourselves negatively watching practice videos. But ignore self-consciousness and look at recordings objectively. Silently observe and take notes as if watching a colleague.
- It minimizes nerves.
  Listening repeatedly reduces fear of hearing your own voice or watching your own mannerisms. Familiarity with your video presence alleviates some stage fright.
- It creates improvement plans.
  Make notes on areas to improve then track progress run to run. Recordings document your growth. Maintain focus by checking in on specific goals.
- It allows review anytime.
  Store practice recordings to replay when convenient rather than relying on memory of sessions. Renew confidence right before go time by watching them.

In summary, recording speeches provides unmatched feedback. It highlights presentation flaws, enables nonverbal and vocal critique, shows content issues, reinforces memorization, checks timing, builds confidence, allows peer input, fosters self-critique, reduces nerves, tracks progress and enables review anytime. Recording devices give the gift of self-reflection. Leverage them to present powerfully.

Get feedback

Crafting a great speech requires more than just practice. You need objective input and critiques from others. Their feedback makes you aware of flaws you cannot see yourself. Do not rely solely on your own judgment. Getting outside perspectives is critical for improvement. Here are key benefits of feedback:

- It provides honesty.
  Friends, colleagues and mentors will honestly critique areas that need work rather than just complimenting you. Take their constructive criticism to heart. They identify gaps you miss while presenting. Welcome this honesty.
- It targets vocal issues.
  Listeners will pinpoint speech problems like speaking too fast, too soft, too monotonous, using fillers, etc. They hear issues your ears tune out. Ask specifically how your vocal delivery sounds to others and take note of their advice.
- It improves body language.
  Observers will comment on distracting mannerisms or movements you are unaware of. Let them critique posture, gestures, fidgeting, eye contact and movement. Do not dismiss their observations. Use it.

- It refines content.
  Feedback will reveal sections that are confusing, overly technical or dry. Listeners will advise where stories wander, or jokes fall flat. They know if conclusions lack impact. Heed their content feedback.
- It provides pacing guidance.
  Observers notice if your pace feels too frantic, sluggish or irregular. Listen to their timing critiques and use a clock to rework pacing. Their outside ears detect pacing problems you miss in the moment.
- It assesses audience connection.
  Feedback reveals if your presentation seems cold and unengaging. Let observers tell you honestly if your speech connected with them emotionally and kept interest levels high. Target weak points.
- It gauges impact.
  Quality feedback tells you which information landed powerfully, and which sections fell flat. Hone in on the most critical data to emphasize based on listener reactions. Focus on what resonated.
- It pinpoints confusing sections.
  If certain concepts or transitions consistently puzzle listeners, rework those spots to enhance clarity. Feedback exposes your blind spots. Clarify wherever confusion arises.

- It checks memorization.
  Observers will note where you repeatedly checked notes or lost your place during practice. Those are areas needing more repetition to strengthen memorization.
- It tracks improvement.
  Thank observers who provide ongoing feedback, not just one-time input. This allows you to chart your progress across multiple rehearsals. Their insights help you grow.

In summary, soldiering on alone leads to blind spots. Relying solely on your own ears and eyes handicaps the refinement process. The more objective feedback you solicit, the stronger your presentation will be. Listen sincerely and respond to advice. Do not rationalize or justify. Strive to improve based on responses. Feedback is a gift enabling growth.

Visualize success

An often overlooked but highly effective technique when gearing up to speak is to visualize giving a successful presentation. Mentally picturing excellence boosts confidence and primes you for the best performance possible. Visualization activates the reticular activating system in the brain, heightening focus and readiness. Here are some key ways visualization succeeds:

- It reinforces content memory.
  Picture yourself presenting smoothly, recalling each point at the right moment. Envision staying on track as you progress seamlessly through sections. This mental rehearsal strengthens neural pathways, improving memory and reducing reliance on notes.
- It boosts confidence.
  Imagining a commanding, engaging presentation with the audience responding positively will make that success feel inevitable. Visualize smiles, nods and applause. Your mind cannot distinguish vivid images from reality, so "see it" and confidence follows.
- It minimizes anxiety.
  Nervous excitement is normal, but anxiety sabotages success. Counter it by picturing yourself feeling grounded, focused and in command on stage. Banish negative visions and loop triumphant mental movies. This calms nerves.

- It improves body language.
  Watch yourself in your mind moving comfortably, maintaining eye contact, speaking with expression, gesturing with purpose, and conveying confidence through posture and stance. Visualize your best physical presentation.
- It refines vocal delivery.
  Hear the ideal version of your voice in your head - projecting clearly, varying tone, using crisp enunciation, speaking conversationally, and avoiding filler words. Your mind rehearses so your voice follows suit.
- It ignites passion.
  Envision yourself speaking with sincere excitement and conviction. Feel your content's importance and see audiences connecting with that enthusiasm. Passion is contagious, so mentally tap into yours before taking the stage.
- It focuses attention.
  Picture external distractions falling away as you maintain total attention on the message and audience. Visualize ignoring disruptions. If you see it, you can achieve it. Mental focus fosters actual focus.
- It prompts adaptability.
  Imagine effortlessly adjusting pacing or emphasis based on audience reactions. See yourself staying fully engaged with the room. Flexibility stems from preparation and visualization reinforces that responsiveness.

- It aligns mental and physical readiness.
  Visualize feeling mentally sharp and physically invigorated prior to speaking. Your body aligns with your mindset. Negating nerves and tapping into energy reserves boosts performance.
- It creates a blueprint for success.
  If you can envision achieving excellence, your subconscious mind works to match that vision. Experiencing something mentally first makes it easier physically. Creative visualization provides the blueprint.

In summary, top athletes, musicians, surgeons, pilots and others visualize success because it works. Harness this technique before public speaking. Picture your presentation going perfectly at all levels. Mental rehearsal primes you for the best outcome. See yourself succeeding and your mind makes sure the body follows that path. Confidence results from imagining victory first.

Chapter 8

Overcoming Stage Fright

Stage fright stops many people from performing well. It doesn't need to. Nerves are an integral part of speeches and presentations. Having a pre presentation routine can really help. Remembering that you are doing this to Connect, Communicate and Convince, can really help you overcome stage fright, as can the following 6 tips.

1. **Prepare**
   Prepare and practice your speech extensively. Knowing your content inside and out will make you feel much more confident and comfortable.

2. **Visualise**
   Visualize yourself giving a successful, smooth speech. See yourself speaking calmly and clearly in your mind.

3. **Breathe**
   Breathe deeply before going on stage. Take some slow, deep breaths to relax and focus yourself.

4. **Connect**
   Connect with the audience. Make eye contact, smile, and speak conversationally to help yourself feel less isolated.

5. **Channel**

   Channel your nervous energy into your delivery.
   Use those butterflies to give you energy and
   enthusiasm.

6. **Focus**

   Focus on your message, not your fears. Keep your
   mind concentrated on conveying your points
   effectively. Don't dwell on your anxieties.

Prepare

For many, speaking in public invokes feelings of anxiety and dread. The body reacts as if under threat, with racing heart, trembling limbs, and thoughts awash in fear. Stage fright can range from mild nerves to paralyzing panic. While some nervousness is natural, excessive anxiety often stems from lack of preparation. Thorough preparation is key to overcoming stage fright in public speaking.

The first step is intimately knowing your material. Craft your speech carefully and be able to explain concepts and ideas clearly. Practice it aloud until your delivery flows smoothly and naturally. Memorize key points rather than the whole speech; impromptu explanations and examples will make you sound more conversational. But have the structure firmly set in your mind. Know your introduction, main points, supporting information, and conclusion.

Visualize giving the speech successfully. See yourself speaking with passion, confidence, and clarity. This mental rehearsal helps install the neural pathways for a positive performance. It also boosts self-efficacy, the belief in your capabilities. Approach the speech with a growth mindset. Focus on developing skills rather than frozen in fear of judgment. Celebrate small wins to build confidence.

Prepare for contingencies that may arise. Consider likely questions the audience may ask and how to respond. Have backup visual aids in case of technical glitches. Prepare to pivot if parts you practiced escape your mind. Accept imperfections and focus forward.

Practice the speech out loud. Imagine responding to distractions, record and listen to yourself, and get feedback to improve. The more you rehearse, the more polished and automatic your delivery will become. As novel tasks become familiar, anxiety diminishes.

Prepare yourself physically as well. Get plenty of rest before your speech so you are energized and focused. Hydrate well and avoid too much caffeine, which can make nerves worse. Breathe deeply to counteract the tight chest of anxiety. Stretch or do light exercise to discharge nervous energy.

Know the audience and venue. Greet attendees as they arrive. Stand where they do to visualize their perspective. Adjust volume and gestures accordingly. Use the stage layout to your advantage. Arrive early to check equipment and layout.

When nervousness strikes, remember that audiences want you to succeed. They are receptive to your message, not critiquing your every move. Channel anxious energy into your delivery, not resisting it. Pause, breathe, and refocus on your intention.

Trust in your hard work. You know this speech backwards and forwards. The content flows logically. You have envisioned succeeding. Focus on communicating your message, not on your fears. Be in the moment; don't distract yourself with past mistakes or future catastrophes. As the saying goes, courage is not the absence of fear, but moving forward despite it.

With extensive preparation of your content, delivery, contingencies and yourself, you can step into that spotlight with confidence. Fully knowing your speech is powerful armour against stage fright. The more you deliberately practice and perform, the more your skills will strengthen. Be patient with the process. Each speech moves you closer to overcoming anxiety and becoming an assured public speaker.

Visualise

Standing in front of an audience giving a presentation invokes fear and anxiety for many people. Palms sweat, voice shakes, mind goes blank. Stage fright can range from mild nerves to paralyzing dread. Visualization is a powerful technique to overcome this phobia. By mentally picturing a successful performance, speakers can install the neural pathways and confidence required for excellence.

Visualization works by priming the mind and body for the desired state. Athletes have long used it to rehearse races and goals. Surgeons visualize procedures prior to operating. Visualization for public speaking should begin weeks before the presentation. Set aside quiet time to sit comfortably, close your eyes, and imagine yourself speaking smoothly and successfully.

Picture the audience listening attentively and responding warmly. Hear the steady tone and cadence of your voice as you fluidly communicate each point. Feel your poised, grounded posture and expansive gestures. Imagine pausing for effect, then continuing with clarity and passion. See yourself connect with individual audience members through eye contact and engaging delivery. Visualize staying centred if questions or issues arise. Feel the sense of satisfaction as you conclude your presentation.

In your mind, make the images realistic, vivid and detailed. Imagine from your own perspective on stage, then watch yourself from the audience. Rehearse getting up to the lectern, arranging your notes, taking a breath, then launching confidently into your introduction. Play it like a movie, in full colour with sounds, scents and physical sensations. If anxiety intrudes, gently release it and redirect to positive images.

Practice this visualization daily to crystallize the neural patterns. As the mind repeats scenarios, the associated neuro-networks strengthen. New nerve paths spur growth of grey matter, laying the infrastructure for accomplished public speaking. This builds fluency and self-assurance. What the brain conceives and believes, it tends to achieve.

Visualization enables you to rehearse the event thoroughly, so you feel immersed in each moment. It closes the gap between concept and physical reality. You have already been there in sensory imagination, increasing familiarity and readiness. There are no surprises on stage because you've rehearsed this scene already in your mind's eye. You gain emotional insulation from anxiety because the experience feels familiar.

A vivid mental walk-through also builds your coping repertoire if things don't go exactly as envisioned. Imagine making errors, then smoothly correcting them. See yourself thinking on your feet when questions arise. Build visualization resilience by practicing minor contingencies. Mental agility transfers to real-time presentations.

The gentle repetition of visualization reprograms your subconscious with positive images, sounds and feelings. Old negative associations fade. New neural networks of calm confidence take root. You are conditioning yourself to enjoy public speaking by linking it to pleasant scenes in your mind. Your brain maps the presentation as safe and successful.

Just before the presentation, visualize the introduction and first few minutes. Step through the scene of taking the stage, arranging your notes, smiling at the audience, then launching clearly into your opening words. You've been here before. When the actual moment arrives, your mind and body know just what to do. The path is laid. You speak from visualization's muscle memory.

With consistent rehearsal in your imagination, you can realize public speaking mastery. Each speech builds your skills and confidence. Visualization creates neural grooves of grace under pressure. You train your mind to be a reservoir of calm from which you can draw strength. You step onto the stage already knowing this scene by heart, prepared to succeed.

Breathe

It's common to feel anxious when facing an audience. Rapid heart rate, trembling limbs, flushing, and breathlessness often accompany stage fright. These fight-or-flight reactions once aided our ancestors against threats. But for modern public speaking, anxiety needs tempering. Often the simplest and most effective way to regulate nerves is by controlling your breathing.

When anxious, people tend to take quick, shallow breaths in the chest. This limits oxygen intake, increasing dizziness, heart rate, and light-headedness. Chest breathing also triggers the sympathetic nervous system, releasing stress hormones like cortisol and adrenaline. Tension accumulates throughout the body.

Diaphragmatic breathing counters this, soothing the nervous system. To practice, place one hand on your chest, the other on your stomach. Inhale slowly through your nose, feeling your belly expand as the diaphragm descends. The chest should stay relatively still. Purse your lips and exhale slowly through your mouth. Your stomach will contract. Repeat for a few minutes until calm.

This abdominal breathing stimulates the parasympathetic nervous system, associated with relaxation. The vagus nerve connects the diaphragm and brain, signalling when you feel safe. As deep breaths massage the vagus nerve, heart rate and blood pressure decrease. Breathing into the belly signals safety to the amygdala, quieting the fear centre of the brain.

As you breathe slowly into your abdomen, close your eyes and envision filling your body with calming light. Imagine breathing out stress, self-doubt and tension. This visualization further soothes your sympathetic nervous system. Tension drains from your muscles as you picture your breath traveling through every cell. Keep breathing consciously until centred and recharged.

Before the presentation, seclude yourself and do a longer breathing session of 10 minutes. Inhale slowly through your nose for a count of 4, hold for 2 counts, then exhale through your mouth for 6 counts. Let any distracting thoughts float by like clouds. Focus only on your breath. Feel your abdomen and ribcage expand like balloons filling up. Then release the breath slowly. Stay present in each breath cycle.

Use this breathing ritual to relax individual muscle groups. As you inhale, envision breathing life into your toes. As you exhale, relax the toes completely. Repeat for the soles, ankles, calves, knees, thighs, pelvis, spine, fingers, wrists, arms, shoulders, neck, jaw, eyes, forehead, and scalp. Feel tensions melting away as you systematically calm each body region.

Just before being introduced, take a final series of deep belly breaths. Send oxygen to every corner of your body, energizing your cells. Visualize breathing confidence and positivity into your heart. Straighten your posture and hold your head high, signalling self-assurance. Roll your shoulders back to open your chest. Feel ready to speak from your diaphragm with resonant depth.

If anxiety creeps up during the presentation, pause subtly and take a slow deep breath. Imagine your breath reaching down through your abdomen and legs into the floor, grounding you. Silently count a few more slow breaths, then continue with conviction. This brief cantering ritual re-collects your poise.

You can also integrate deep breathing techniques into your speech to maximize presence. Inhale gently before making an important point, allowing you to speak from your calm centre. When Facilitating audience participation, breathe slowly while listening to questions, then exhale before responding. Insert conscious pauses where appropriate to breathe deeply and gather your thoughts.

Remember that most audiences cannot detect a speaker's internal state when breathing appears controlled. Maintaining poised rhythmic breaths portrays outer confidence, regardless of inner nerves. With discipline, anxiety can fuel expressiveness rather than freeze it. Conscious breathing transforms nerves into vitality.

Breath control provides a powerful tool to overcome stage fright before or during presentations. By mastering the breath, speakers master themselves. Even a few minutes of abdominal breathing activates relaxation and concentration. With practice, anxious presentations become mindful opportunities to connect from your authentic self. Your breath anchors you in the present, focused on sharing your passion with others.

Connect

Public speaking makes many people shrink inside themselves, gripped in the spotlight. But building connection with your audience can dramatically ease stage fright. Human interaction invokes our innate social capacities and eases isolating fears. Fostering a rapport makes listeners receptive to your message and less judgmental if you make mistakes. Focusing on your audience helps quiet inner critics.

Begin connecting before you even take the stage. If possible, arrive early and mingle casually with attendees as they enter. Greet people, make eye contact, and converse light-heartedly. This allows you to engage attendees as fellow humans, not faceless judges. Starting conversations in a low-pressure context first builds familiarity.

Open your speech by welcoming everyone warmly. Thank them for their time and interest in the topic. Keep your tone conversational, like you're addressing a room of friends. This framing lays the groundwork for a dialogue, not a judgmental monologue.

Read the audience's energy and subtly adjust your pace, tone or examples accordingly. Insert humour when they seem reserved, or get more serious if they become too casual. Adapt to keep them attentive, without losing continuity. This live feedback loop makes the speech reciprocal.

Weave in examples relevant to this group so your points resonate uniquely. Reference individuals in the room or local sites when appropriate. Shape content to their interests and concerns. This shows you relate to their context and tailored your message just for them.

Invite and listen to audience comments to spark organic interaction. Be attentive and fully present as they speak. Make eye contact and thank them enthusiastically for participating. Their involvement will make you both more comfortable, knowing you're in a dialogue.

If you feel nervousness swelling, pause to connect sincerely with one audience member. Make eye contact and focus intently on their face for a few seconds, appreciating their presence. This mental time-out redirects your attention from inner worries to an external human connection. Then carry on calmly.

Notice audience reactions so you can adjust your delivery accordingly. If you seem to be losing people, liven up your energy and insert vibrant examples. If they appear overwhelmed, slow your pace and simplify explanations. Adapt in real time based on the feedback they provide.

After your speech, mingle with attendees again. Ask for their impressions, feedback and lingering questions. Address them by name and keep conversing casually after the formal presentation. This underscores your shared humanity and interest in interacting beyond rigid roles.

Approach public speaking as an act of sharing, not performing. Mindset shapes reality, so emphasize communicating, not impressing. You have knowledge others want to learn. Focus on fulfilling their needs, not judging yourself. This collective purpose eases self-consciousness.

Remember most audiences are receptive to speakers and want them to do well. They're not scrutinizing your every move, but are there to learn from you. Framing listeners as collaborators rather than critics helps overcome stage fright. You're all on the same team.

Of course, connection requires projecting confidence and authority appropriate for the venue. But done sincerely, it humanizes public speaking. Fostering dialogue makes the experience more intimate and frames your message as a gift, not a lecture. Instead of isolation, you feel intimate community.

By bookending your talk with casual interaction, maintaining eye contact, adapting to feedback, inviting participation, and conveying interest in your audience as individuals, you transform impersonal performance into meaningful human exchange. The chemistry of connection can convert stage fright into courage to share your passion with people who want to hear it.

Channel

It's natural to feel anxious speaking publicly. Your heart pounds, palms sweat, mind races - the classic fight-or-flight response. These symptoms of stage fright can seem like your body hijacking your poised image. But rather than fighting nerves, you can channel that energy into an asset.

Nervousness before presentations is the activation of mental and physical resources to meet a demand. Your body is ramping up to help you perform under pressure. Evolutionarily, elevated heart rate boosted blood flow to muscles so our ancestors could run from predators. For modern speeches, you can redirect that rush to enhance your delivery.

First, reframe anxiety as excitement. The physiological sensations are virtually identical - fluttering stomach, adrenaline surge, racing thoughts. So consciously choose to interpret them positively before taking the stage. Tell yourself you are eager to share your message, not dreading judgment.

As you feel nervousness building, take some slow deep breaths. Purposefully send that vigour down into your belly. Visualize your restless energy flowing like electricity through your core, energizing your body. Your passion rises within.

Practice channelling that intensity into your posture. Straighten your spine, hold your head high, and stand tall. Let adrenaline boost your stature so you fill the stage with confidence. Widen your stance slightly and balance your weight to feel grounded yet agile.

Make strong eye contact with a sense of boldness fuelled by your nerves. Scan the room purposefully, really seeing each person. Avoid darting eyes that betray anxiety. Channel your apprehension into direct, meaningful connection.

Speak clearly and audibly from your diaphragm, using nervous momentum to project dynamically. Tap your anxiety to add volume and carrying capacity to your voice. Enunciate each word crisply.

Use hand gestures bigger and more energetically than normal conversation. Flow that tense electricity into expressive movements. Gesticulate with passion, channelling restless energy outward to engage the audience. Avoid stiff or trembling hands by infusing them with purpose.

Involve your whole body in presenting, moving dynamically around the stage. Use nervous urges to propel you fluidly as you speak, not rooted tensely in one spot. Walk assertively to different spots, pivoting gracefully to address the room.

Insert dramatic pauses where appropriate, then resume speaking with intensity. Allow extra time for listeners to process important points. Heighten anticipation by using your anxious vibes to charge the silence. Time pauses confidently rather than rushing nervously.

Modulate your voice dynamically, using highs and lows for emphasis. Let your adrenaline push your voice beyond its average plateau. Stress key words and phrases using vocal variety. Passion fuels expression.

Respond to audience reactions with dexterity, smoothly adjusting your pace or tone. Use those nerves to think on your feet. Welcome the energy to improvise explanations or examples. Extemporize with confidence.

If you do stumble, pause and take a breath. Channel your nerves into concentration to quickly recover. Then continue smoothly, using your momentum. Don't freeze or withdraw. Keep your delivery energized.

Close with strength and conviction, fuelled by the anticipation of finishing. Use any remaining nervousness to powerfully deliver your concluding message. End memorably and dynamically.

With practice, you can transform stage fright into vitality and presence. The key is not resisting anxiety but redirecting it. Embrace the sensations and intentionally channel them into delivery. Turn nerves that might have once paralyzed you into the electricity that lights up your speech. You don't conquer stage fright - you unleash its power.

Focus

Speaking publicly makes even confident people nervous. Anxiety is an evolutionary response alerting us to potential threats in the environment. But for modern presentations, these fears are exaggerated in our minds. The key is learning to curb a wandering mind and remain focused on your goals. Intention and concentration can overcome stage fright.

In the days leading up to a presentation, mentally concentrate on your desire to positively impact the audience. Visualize their faces illuminated with understanding as you convey ideas meaningfully. Envision the satisfaction of seeing concepts connect. This plants seeds of purpose that can blossom in the moment.

To quell last minute jitters, sit quietly backstage and meditate briefly. Focus solely on your breath, picturing stress leaving your body on each outward exhale. Silently repeat an affirming mantra like "I am calm and confident." Visualize yourself speaking smoothly. This meditation centres the mind away from distracting fears.

Just before being introduced, pause to consciously focus your motivation. Connect again with your sincerely held wish to inform or inspire the audience. The spotlight awaits your message. Reaffirm your belief in its value. Let this purpose eclipse self-doubt.

As you take the stage, pause silently to survey the audience with appreciation. Make eye contact and connect with a few individuals, focusing your attention outward. Take a breath and smile subtly to ground yourself in the present before speaking.

When anxious thoughts intrude during a presentation, gently direct your concentration back to your message. Ignore worries and self-judgment. Refocus on conveying the next point clearly. The audience wants to learn from you - meet their needs.

Insert impromptu thoughts or examples relevant to this specific group. Tailoring your content keeps you immersed in the immediacy of their experience. Don't dwell on past mistakes or future troubles stay focused on your audience's here-and-now.

If you do stumble or forget your place, avoid dwelling on it. Pause, regroup, take a breath and move forward. Keeping your focus forward prevents anxiety snowballing. Audiences empathize with miscues that are quickly recovered.

Focus intently on listening anytime audience members speak or ask questions. Give them your complete attention, making eye contact and expressing gratitude for their participation. This keeps you engaged.

When nerves strike, focus deliberately on slowing your breathing. Inhale deeply and visualize sending oxygen throughout your body. Exhale slowly while thinking of your breath circulating everywhere. This is calming.

Maintain focus on communicating concepts rather than judging yourself. Get out of your head and into the experience. Make eye contact, speak expressively, and stay present. Immerse in conveying ideas, not evaluating.

Close your speech by making sustained eye contact with the audience. Thank them for their attention, and stay focused on their faces as they applaud, not your churning thoughts. Keep centred on the people before you.

With consistent practice over time, the anxiety triggered by public speaking will diminish. But in the moment, careful focus provides an anchor against stage fright. Redirecting attention from fear to purpose prevents nervous thoughts looping out of control.

When we ruminate on worries and judge ourselves, anxiety escalates. But by tenaciously focusing outward on your audience and message, you can find calm in the storm. Concentration calms turbulent minds and emotions. Rather than fighting nerves, flow with them by staying immersed in each unfolding moment. Speak from your still centre.

Chapter 9

Impromptu Speaking Skills

Speaking of the cuff, extemporaneous or impromptu speaking is often thought to be one of the most difficult speaking skills. It can be difficult, but done well, it can be one of the best ways to Connect, Communicate and Convince. The following 6 tips will help you greatly with this.

1. **Think**
    Take a moment to collect your thoughts before starting. Pause, take a breath, and think about your main point.

2. **Keep it Real**
    Stick to what you know. Draw from your areas of knowledge and experience to speak comfortably. Don't ramble beyond your expertise.

3. **Keep it simple.**
    Have one key message or story that conveys your main idea in a focused, memorable way.

4. **End well**
    Have a clear ending. Wrap up with a summary statement circling back to your original point. Ending decisively gives the impromptu remarks shape.

5. **Listen**

   Listen closely. Make sure you fully understand the
   question or prompt before responding so your
   answer is relevant. Ask clarifying questions if needed.

6. **Structure**

   Follow a structure. Even when improvising, follow an
   organizational pattern like chronological order or
   problem-solution format.

Think

Being put on the spot to speak publicly without preparation can be intimidating. Taking a moment to intentionally collect your thoughts is key to delivering clear impromptu remarks. Mental composure enables coherent communication even when caught off guard.

When faced with an unexpected question or prompt, avoid rushing to respond immediately. Instead, use a phrase to discreetly buy some time to get centred, such as "That's an excellent question, let me think for a moment..." or "I need to reflect on that idea for a second before responding..."

As you briefly pause externally, turn your focus inward to evaluate the situation. What type of response is required here? Does the prompt relate to your knowledge base? Taking a few seconds for this initial assessment allows you to determine the optimal direction.

Next, clarify the question or prompt internally before proceeding. Make sure you fully understand what is being asked. If anything is unclear, politely ask for the speaker to elaborate or rephrase. Misinterpreting the prompt will derail your whole response.

Breathing deeply also helps collect your thoughts and ease any flare up of anxiety. Inhale slowly from your abdomen, visualizing the breath traveling through your body. Exhale completely. Repeat this a few times until you feel centred and calm. Oxygen will fuel your brain.

Mentally scan your knowledge and experience for relevant content to address the question or topic. Draw upon what you know related to the subject area. Gather examples, statistics, anecdotes, and key ideas that correspond.

Catalogue these mental resources and consider how to organize them into a coherent structure. Should you layout strengths then weaknesses? Chronological order? Problem then solution? Choose a logical flow to build your impromptu framework. Jot down visual cues on paper if needed.

Distil your message down to a few concise key points that get right to the heart of the matter. Impromptu remarks should be brief and focused. Let peripheral details fall away to keep the core ideas clear. Less is more.

Phrase an opening sentence in your mind that clearly sets up your impromptu response. Start strongly with a relevant statement or thought-provoking question to orient the audience. End your remarks with a memorable concluding sentence that synthesizes the main ideas.

Visualize yourself speaking slowly, smoothly and confidently as you verbally convey your organized thoughts. Picture connecting with the audience through eye contact and clear delivery. This mental rehearsal provides a model to follow.

When ready to respond, take a final deep breath to infuse calm energy through your body. Make eye contact with a sense of grounded presence. After your opening statement, pause briefly between impromptu points to stay thoughtful and centred.

Being able to think on your feet requires mental composure. Avoid feeling flustered or frozen when an unexpected question arises. Instead, leverage techniques to collect yourself internally. Communicating skilfully relies first on a composed mind.

With practice over time, you can develop greater comfort with impromptu remarks. But even seasoned speakers get rattled when put on the spot. The key is using this brief inner retreat to ground yourself in the moment before speaking. External poise originates from internal stillness.

When pressure hits, the capacity to collect your thoughts is invaluable. By mastering the mental space around moments of impromptu speech, you master the moments themselves. With poise and preparation, you can convey ideas as precisely spontaneously as from a script.

Keep it real

Being put on the spot to speak without preparation can rattle anyone. But falling back on your existing expertise is a proven way to deliver clear impromptu remarks. Drawing from your wheelhouse provides a comfort zone to minimize anxiety and maximize coherent communication.

When faced with an unexpected public speaking prompt, resist any urge to bluff your way through alien subject matter. Attempting to discuss unfamiliar topics increases the odds of floundering. Instead, keep your responses squarely within your established knowledge base.

Take a moment to breathe and reflect on the question or topic presented. Evaluate if this relates clearly to your background, experiences, skills or interests. If so, you have abundant firsthand material to pull from to craft an intelligent response.

For example, a scientist asked to comment about her research specialty can share details about experiments, data, and insights from years of immersive study. A retired teacher questioned about education policy can cite real classroom challenges and best practices.

When the subject corresponds to your expertise, confidently shape your impromptu remarks around what you know best. Don't hesitate to reference technical terms, data points, historical context, practical examples and anecdotes. Your knowledge gives you the liberty to go deep.

If only part of the question or topic aligns with your strengths, focus your response entirely on those relevant portions. You don't need to address every aspect. It's smarter to elaborate fully on what you know well rather than superficially cover unfamiliar terrain.

Of course, be careful not to get overly pedantic with impromptu responses. Keep in mind the audience and their level of knowledge about your specialty. Make sure to explain complex concepts clearly. Define unfamiliar jargon. Distil details to be digestible yet meaningful.

When responding off-the-cuff, stick to broad principles and your most compelling material to keep remarks focused. Resist the urge to exhaustively recount every factoid you know, which can muddle messages. Remember - concision, relevance and clarity are key.

Backing up opinions with facts and statistics from your profession adds credibility. But ensure accuracy by mentally double-checking numbers as you speak. Citing incorrect data under pressure could undermine your authority, especially if fact-checked later. When in doubt, avoid specifics.

Use personal anecdotes judiciously to make impromptu responses relatable, but keep them concise. For instance, a teacher could briefly reference interacting with a struggling student to humanize a point about empathy, then tie it back to the broader discussion.

When sharing off-the-cuff, occasionally confirm the audience is following your sentiments. Ask if examples are resonating or if more context would be helpful. This live feedback ensures you stay on track.

With practice, you can become adept at impromptu speaking within your circle of competence. Draw confidence from mastering facts, ideas and experiences. Lean on this bedrock knowledge to steady any remarks delivered under pressure. Your expertise provides the foundation to stand tall.

From technical briefings to candid interviews, the ability to speak intelligently without preparation is an invaluable skill. Mastery requires identifying your knowledge sweet spots and playing to these strengths when put on the spot. Stick to what you know best and let your experience guide you.

Keep it simple

When caught off guard by a public speaking prompt, our tendency is to ramble in order to fill uncomfortable silences. But conveying complex ideas clearly under pressure requires the discipline of simplicity. Impromptu remarks should distil messages down to the most salient points.

Limit your spontaneous responses to 1-3 key themes or narratives. This crystallizes your message and avoids confusing audiences with disjointed overload. If you only have one great point relevant to the topic, focus on elaborating and illustrating that point artfully. One profound insight is more memorable than a dozen shallow observations.

For instance, if asked to comment impromptu on ways to conserve energy, stick to your most actionable advice. Perhaps suggest setting thermostats 2 degrees cooler in winter and higher in summer as the simplest high-impact tactic. Rather than listing every conservation tip you know, provide one clear takeaway.

When crafting your main points, use vivid examples, metaphors or stories to paint the core ideas in bold relief. For instance, liken cutting food waste to eliminating several unnecessary daily trips to the grocery store. This conjures a tangible image that resonates more than abstract facts. Creative analogies make messages stick.

Follow the KISS principle - Keep It Simple, Smarty. Resist the urge to pepper responses with obscure jargon or technical minutiae just because you know them. While expertise should inform content, ensure terms are broadly understandable. Explain concepts at an accessible level.

Similarly, keep number usage judicious and round figures for easy recall. For example, saying the average family spends £280 per month on electricity conveys the point just fine. Precisely quantifying £278.63 may impress but won't be retained. Err toward approximations when improvising.

Sound bites also work. A memorable one-liner capturing your central theme makes a strong impromptu response. For instance: "An ounce of prevention is worth a pound of cure." This pithy proverb eloquently answers a question about prioritizing disease prevention.

Avoid convoluted sentence structure when speaking off the cuff. Use simple subject-verb patterns that are straightforward to parse and follow. Your goal is clarity amid complexity. Plainspoken language comes off more assured than tangled verbosity.

Repetition of key terms also brings cohesion to impromptu remarks. For example, frequently reference the core concept of "health equity" when imploring action on disparities. Repeating this mantra cements understanding and underscores the central theme.

Close impromptu responses decisively with a clear summary statement circling back to your original point. For instance: "In the end, promoting exercise delivers compounding dividends across communities." This clinches the takeaway.

With practice, you can develop an ability to simplify and distil even while handling curveball questions or tasks. Impromptu speaking relies on conveying one compelling point people remember over peripheral details forgotten. Keeping responses focused, vivid and digestible will ensure your message sticks.

End well

Masterful communication means leading your audience on a journey that arrives purposefully at a destination. This holds true even for impromptu speaking when remarks must be crafted on the fly. A clear ending provides closure and drives home the central point, elevating disjointed rambling into poised persuasion.

An effectual closing statement for off-the-cuff responses should summarize key themes into a unified message using different phrasing. Repetition reinforces retention. Echo the overall position without redundancy. For instance, restate the importance of "fiscal prudence and saving" as "living within our means."

The ending should contextualize the broader implications of the prompt. For example, after improvising about methods to reduce food waste, the closing line could be: "Small daily changes by each of us would significantly lessen environmental degradation." This thematic wrap-up elevates the specific issue to its larger meaning.

When possible, tie back to your opening statement or an engaging anecdote used during impromptu remarks. This creates symmetry, reminding audiences of compelling ideas raised initially. Brief callbacks give speeches structural coherence.

Audiences also appreciate hearing clear conclusions providing guidance on next steps. Your final sentence should suggest practical actions, priorities going forward, or questions for further thought. Impromptu remarks should enlighten audiences beyond the moment.

For instance, after urging workplace mentoring programs, conclude with: "Let's reflect on ways we can lift each other up then put those into practice." Or ask, "How could we implement peer support in our own organization?"

Even when time is limited, do more than trail off or merely thank the audience at the end. Push yourself to crystallize an impactful, unifying conclusion rather than stopping abruptly. Ending strong frames you as decisive.

However, don't artificially stretch out a closing just to fill time. If you've conveyed the essence completely, a simple powerful statement may suffice: "Let's have the courage to do what's right." Quality trumps quantity.

Word choice also matters greatly. Ending on a concept central to your main idea sticks meaning. Perhaps that one word is "integrity" or "empathy" or "perseverance." Let this final vocabulary encapsulate your theme.

Without a clear ending providing summation and guidance, impromptu remarks can feel disjointed. Audiences need synthesis and perspective. Your role as a speaker is not just to introduce ideas but also provide a conclusion making sense of it all.

Even professional speakers only hit persuasive endings occasionally through practice. But in the impromptu moment, aiming for coherence and resonance sets you up to stick the landing. With time and experience, your clarity and confidence will grow.

Think of a memorable ending line as the bow that neatly wraps up an imperfect impromptu package. Though the contents may seem hastily wrapped, a perfect bow makes a beautiful present. Put in the effort for impactful closure.

Remaining mindful of the finish line throughout your impromptu response allows you to lay the groundwork for a smooth landing. Keep circling back mentally to how you'll synthesize it all. Then craft a final statement sending audiences away with clarity, conviction and next steps. Your improvised remarks will spark inspiration that lasts far beyond the last word.

Listen

Impromptu speaking relies heavily on careful listening. Failing to fully grasp the question or prompt inevitably derails your response. Listening intently from the outset allows you to shape astute remarks that directly meet the needs of the moment.

When faced with an unexpected public speaking assignment, avoid assuming you understand the question or jumping to formulate an answer. Even if pressed for time, make focused listening your priority.

If the question or instructions are at all ambiguous, politely ask for clarification or rephrasing before responding. Eliminate any doubt about context or expectations. Misinterpreting the premise sends your whole impromptu speech astray.

As the question is being posed, maintain eye contact and open body language with the speaker. Nod periodically to confirm you are tracking. Avoid interrupting or trying to anticipate where it's leading. Simply absorb.

Echo the main points back verbally to verify comprehension if feasible. For instance, paraphrase: "If I'm understanding correctly, you are asking about ways to...X. Is that an accurate summary?" This extra step gets you started correctly.

Listen between the lines for nuances and implications beyond the literal question. For instance, does the person seem concerned about specific risks or hoping for an inspirational perspective? Adjust your angle accordingly.

If responding to a complex multi-part question, tactfully ask which aspect should be your focus. Listening for clues about priorities will prevent wasting time on peripheral issues.

When listening, jot down key terms on paper or take mental notes. Identifying core vocabulary helps retrieve relevant background knowledge to address the topic. These captured keywords spark ideas.

Avoid formulating your reply while others are still speaking. Honor their words by focusing all mental energy on comprehending. Crafting an agenda while listening guarantees missing subtleties.

After responding, circle back soliciting any clarification about your interpretation. Ask "Did I address your specific question effectively?" Feedback ensures you didn't miss the mark.

Listening intently upfront also buys processing time to organize thoughtful responses. Nodding attentively signals you are thoughtfully absorbing the question, not simply freezing.

Reflect the speaker's terminology and tone in your response when appropriate. Matching vocabulary fosters connection and signals close listening. If they seem casual or formal, you adapt respectively.

Most importantly, listen with sincerity and presence, not just waiting to talk. Fully tune in to the speaker's sentiments and motivation in asking. Understanding the humanity behind questions leads to relevance and rapport.

Additionally, listen closely to audience reactions as you speak. Perceive their energy and nonverbal cues. Are they engaged? Confused? Bored? Adjust your content and delivery accordingly.

Impromptu speaking relies heavily on skilfully understanding the prompt and listener needs in real time. Before rushing to fill silence, devote complete focus to closely absorbing questions. Listening is the foundation on which meaningful responses are constructed.

With consistent practice, your ability to listen under pressure will improve. Cultivate patience with ambiguity and avoid knee-jerk reactions. Composure enables comprehension. Leverage listening to ensure your off-the-cuff remarks hit home for audiences, meeting the heart of each unique situation.

Structure

While impromptu speaking requires thinking on your feet, having a structured framework keeps your remarks coherent. Organizing, even briefly, helps connect disparate thoughts into a logical flow. Following an orderly model prevents free association that can confuse audiences.

When faced with an unexpected prompt, quickly choose a foundational structure to guide your response. Useful formats include chronological order, problem-solution, compare-contrast, pros-cons, cause-effect and others. Pick a sequence suitable to the topic.

For instance, if asked to discuss challenges facing small businesses, a problem-solution format lends itself well. Outline two or three key problems first, then propose corresponding solutions. This progression makes intuitive sense to listeners.

Or if asked to describe your education path, a chronological structure starting from early schooling moving forward provides an easy spine. Briefly highlight formative moments building one upon the next.

Make mental notes or quick jots mapping the progression of your main points. Having this bird's-eye view, even if hastily sketched, keeps your impromptu train on track. Don't wander aimlessly.

Open your response clearly announcing the organizing principle upfront: "I'll address this by walking through problems first, then solutions." Explicitly naming your structure orients the audience. They will anticipate next steps.

To ensure coherence, use consistent transitional phrases as guideposts when moving between sections: First, Second, Next, Finally, Consequently, Therefore, etc. Verbal signposts bring fluency.

Vary the length and complexity of sentences throughout the impromptu response to maintain interest. Follow short crisp points with fuller explanations. Contrast long elaborate phrasing with punchy one-liners.

Reinforce structure by periodically referring back to main headings: "So in summary that covers our two biggest challenges: lack of resources and team fatigue. Now let's explore corresponding solutions."

Close by circling back to your opening framework statement. For instance: "In the end, walking through causes then effects illuminated factors behind the trends." Bookending brings satisfying closure.

Beyond core formats, consider creative models to bring life to impromptu responses. Organize remarks as a fictitious dialogue, a mock news report, the unfolding of a mystery, or a journey with milestones.

Visual people can improvise using a mental whiteboard, chalkboard, slides, or even physical space, gesturing spatially to place points. Use your natural talents.

With practice over time, organizational frameworks become second nature, lending structure to any impromptu situation. But in the heat of the moment, having even a simple consistency model prevents disjointed rambling.

Of course, the content, examples and delivery must connect with audiences, not just the format. But an extemporaneous speech without coherent form risks leaving listeners confused. An organized flow channels ideas for clarity and conviction.

Next time you face an unexpected question or prompt, embrace the creative challenge to craft thoughtful structure quickly. With poise and preparation, you can build order around even impromptu chaos. Frameworks frame understanding. Give your audiences stepping stones to walk along with you toward insight.

Chapter 10

Handling Q & A Sessions Confidently

You've given your speech. It has gone exceptionally well.
Now is the time to really Connect, Communicate and
Convince. We can do that through our Q & A session.
Rember to put the Q & A session, just prior to your summary
and call to action, so that you are the last person the
audience hear. When it is time for the Q & A these 6 tips will
help you to navigate it successfully.

1. **Manage**
   Manage the Q & A process confidently. Repeat
   questions for the full audience to hear. Ensure one
   person speaks at a time. Close the Q & A session
   smoothly when time is up.

2. **Anticipate**
   Anticipate likely questions and prepare responses in
   advance. Consider the topics you covered and what
   may need clarification. Practice answering out loud.

3. **Listen**
   Listen carefully to each question before responding.
   Make sure you fully understand what is being asked.
   Repeat or paraphrase the question to confirm.

4. **Eye contact**

    Make eye contact with the person asking the
    question. Thank them for the question and refer to
    them by name, if possible, to make it more personal.

5. **Pause**

    Don't feel like you must answer immediately. Pause
    briefly to consider your response if needed. Silence is
    OK.

6. **Clear and concise**

    Keep responses clear and concise. Focus on the
    essence of the question rather than rambling. It's fine
    to say you don't know something and will follow up
    later.

Manage

The Question & Answer period is a free-flowing conversation, but as presenter you must steer it with confidence and care. Manage the Q & A discreetly to ensure coherence, inclusion and clear communication for the benefit of all. Your leadership enables meaningful dialogue.

To start, explain the Q & A process and expectations upfront before taking questions. Explain if questions should be held to the end or interspersed. Ask attendees to raise hands and wait for the microphone which you will monitor and distribute. This primes participants to engage constructively.

When recognizing questioners, establish eye contact first, if possible, to make connection before they speak. Thank them and refer to them by name if known. This gives a human touch to balance the formality of queued speaking.

Repeat or paraphrase questions out loud before answering so everyone can hear the full context clearly. If you summarize, confirm accuracy with the original asker. This loop prevents misinterpretation.

Manage the pace by selecting about 2-3 substantial questions to dive into rather than rapid-fire shallow responses. Judge which questions will yield the most meaningful discussion for the full audience. Go deep.

If needed, remind the room that you would like one person speaking at a time so answers can be heard. Politely intercept sidebar conversations or interruptions. Keep the environment focused.

Watch time closely as the Q & A proceeds. Wrap up question intake about 5 minutes before the allotted Q & A time ends. Then briefly answer 1-2 final questions teed up. Plan a definitive ending.

Close the session by thanking everyone for their excellent questions and highlighting key themes or takeaways from the discussion. If needed, apologize for any unanswered questions and offer follow-up contact.

For conferences with large audiences, conference organizers may screen and select questions ahead of time to ensure coherence. But still prepare to manage spontaneous follow-ups.

For virtual events, monitor incoming questions from the chat or Q & A box. Verbally restate questions before responding for the audience's benefit. Doing so allows filtering inappropriate questions.

If hostile or irrelevant questions arise, answer politely and briefly, then redirect to a different person. Defuse confusion or tensions through calm redirection rather than confrontation.

The Q & A offers great reward but requires facilitation. Confidently guide the ship through potential rough waters. With experience, you will handle diverse questions and dynamics smoothly. Your leadership powers the Q & A.

Anticipate

Questions inevitably arise when audiences don't fully grasp concepts or want more detail on topics covered. Savvy speakers mentally prepare likely queries in advance rather than being caught off guard. Anticipating post-presentation questions allows thoughtful, confident responses.

First, carefully review your presentation content and flow. Make a list of key points along with supporting facts, research, examples and explanations. These are prime targets for audience questions. Ask yourself: What needs elaboration? Where might confusion arise?

For instance, if you quote statistics, be ready to cite exact sources and methodology if scrutinized. For conceptual points, have clear definitions and metaphors ready to clarify. For proposals, anticipate probes about implementation challenges.

During the presentation, make note if listeners seem particularly engaged with certain points. Passions and perplexed expressions signal content requiring follow up. Adjust your expectations for questions accordingly.

Consider your audience's knowledge level on the topic. A novice group may ask more basic clarification questions about fundamentals. Experts will want to explore nuances, implications, and omissions. Tailor preparation accordingly.

Factor in audience demographics too. For instance, financial analysts may zero in on ROI projections while engineers question technical specs. Teachers may ask about classroom applications. Consider what each cohort cares about most.

Prepare for commonly asked queries appropriate for the topic such as: Why is this important? How does this impact me? What should I do differently? Can you elaborate on risks? What's your evidence base? Anticipate these broader themes.

Have handy analogies, anecdotes and additional examples ready to explain complex processes and ideas simply if needed. Visuals also help convey multilayered topics clearly when summarized verbally.

Practice answering likely questions out loud to sharpen your responses. Get feedback from colleagues playing Devil's advocate. Refine and simplify your language. Listen to your recorded answers to improve.

If anticipating a controversial subject, plan responses that acknowledge and validate all perspectives. Don't disparage other views. Frame your position thoughtfully. Admit limitations where appropriate.

Prepare follow-up actions for deeper questions you can't address fully in the Q & A timeframe. Offer to provide resources, references, or individual outreach. This shows you are taking their inquiry seriously.

No one can anticipate every possible curveball question. If caught unprepared, say you appreciate the question and will follow up with them afterward. Don't improvise answers that may be inaccurate.

Have your presentation materials on hand during Q & A to reference if needed. But avoid reading directly from slides, which looks disengaged. Maintain eye contact.

The more presentations you give, the better you will become at forecasting audience queries. You'll develop intuition for which points will require elaboration. Then Q & A becomes conversation, not interrogation. Think ahead.

Listen

The Q & A session provides opportunity for clarity, depth and connection with your audience. But fulfil its potential by truly listening to each query. Avoid assumptions and give your complete attention. Embrace questions as collaboration, not confrontation.

Start by thanking the person for their question and repeating or paraphrasing it to confirm your understanding. For example, "Let me make sure I understand your question. You are asking about our timeline for..." This reflective listening technique ensures you don't miss the mark if your interpretation is off.

Focus completely on comprehending each questioner by maintaining eye contact and adopting open, engaged body language. Ignore any audience members calling out other questions simultaneously. Tune in only to the current speaker.

Especially for remote presentations, ask follow up questions if the initial question seems vague or fragmented. Say: "I want to make sure I fully understand your question before responding. Could you please elaborate a bit more on X aspect?"

Listen between the lines for the motivation and assumptions underlying questions. Is someone sceptical of your data, confused about applications, or hoping for a specific answer? Perceiving these subtleties allows you to tailor helpful responses.

Avoid mentally formulating your reply while the person is still speaking. Honor their effort by listening with your full mental focus. Don't just wait for your turn to talk over them. Deep listening builds rapport.

If faced with a multi-part question, tactfully ask the speaker to prioritize which aspect they would like you to focus on first given time constraints. This ensures you address their highest concern rather than wasting time on peripherals.

Take notes on key points from lengthy queries you want to address in your response. Especially for remote presentations, you won't have eye contact or body language cues to prompt your memory as well. Write down critical terminology.

Listen for common themes and root issues arising across different questions and attendees. Identify where misunderstandings, doubts or enthusiasm converge so you can address systemically.

After responding, check in with the original questioner briefly to see if you fully resolved their query. Ask "Did I address your question fully?" or "Is there any aspect you would like me to elaborate further on?" This follow-through demonstrates sincere listening.

If speaker time expires before you can fully address a question, apologize for the constraint and offer to follow up with them individually afterward. Make it clear that you respect their contribution.

Close the Q & A by summarizing common threads and key takeaways you heard across all questions. This underscores your commitment to listening to your audience's voice, not just conveying one-way content.

Thoughtful, attentive listening transforms Q & A sessions from cursory obligation to rich dialogue. Audiences offer valuable insights when we truly open our ears. Each question is an opportunity to clarify, connect and collaborate. Make sure your listening does justice to their effort in asking.

Eye contact

The Q & A period following a presentation allows deeper audience engagement through conversation. Speakers should facilitate this dialogue by making deliberate eye contact with each person addressing them. This nonverbal cue conveys presence, interest and respect.

When someone stands to ask a question, immediately look directly at them as they speak. Maintain consistent eye contact to signal your complete attention is focused on comprehending their words. Avoid scanning the room or looking down at your notes.

Making eye contact visibly demonstrates active listening. The speaker feels seen and heard. Your eye connection encourages them to elaborate on details and feel relaxed interacting. This sets a thoughtful tone for exchange.

Without eye contact, audience members may feel ignored or that you are disinterested in their contribution. Speakers who look around the room or down at notes appear distracted and disengaged. The questioner deserves your full visual focus.

For remote video presentations, look directly into your camera when responding to capture eye contact through the virtual medium. Position your camera near the monitor so your gaze remains centred on the participant's image. This simulates in-person interaction.

When addressing the question out loud for the full room, maintain eye contact with the original asker rather than scanning the whole audience. Keep the conversational flow between you and that person intact.

If on a stage, walk closer to the questioner to further close the literal and metaphoric distance. Eliminate any sense of disconnect. This physical gesture underscores your interest in their perspective.

To foster even deeper connection, address them by name if you know it from registration or introductions. Thank "Maria" or "John" for the excellent question. Using names personalizes the exchange.

After your response, return to making eye contact and ask if you fully answered their question or if they would like you to elaborate further. This eye connection continues the back-and-forth flow.

If the question comes from a hostile or confrontational place, maintain eye contact to show openness and confidence. Do not show weakness by looking away.

However, avoid aggressive staring or prolonged eye contact after your response, which could seem intimidating or aggressive. Return to scanning the full audience until the next question arises.

Making human-to-human eye contact amid group presentations fosters community and rapport. The Q & A period offers these intimate moments to turn impersonal lectures into meaningful conversations.

Even large audiences will feel you relating to them individually when you give presence through consistent eye contact. Faces become real people, not just indistinct crowds. Eye connection builds trust and understanding.

With the prevalence of remote speaking, using your webcam to make "eye contact" must be an intentional practice. But this simulated gaze fosters essential community and dialogue. Looking into the camera is looking into their eyes.

Q & A eye contact acknowledges audience effort in asking questions and conveys your openness to dissenting perspectives. With patience and practice, organic dialogue can emerge from this shared visual foundation. Eye contact humanizes public speaking.

Pause

When faced with audience questions after a presentation, the natural instinct is to respond immediately. However, allowing a pause before addressing each query projects poise and ensures coherent answers. Embrace silence to collect your thoughts.

As soon as a question is asked, avoid blurting out the first idea that crosses your mind. Even if put on the spot, it is acceptable to take time formulating your thoughts before speaking. Silence does not betray ignorance.

In fact, verbally acknowledge that you will take a moment before providing your answer. For example: "That's an excellent question. Let me take a second to think through my response." This lets the audience know the delay reflects care in your answer, not lack of one.

During the pause, maintain eye contact with the questioner rather than looking down or away. Nod in acknowledgment and appreciation as you gather your thoughts. This sustains engagement in the silence.

If put on the spot, rephrase the question out loud first. This vocal repetition buys some processing time while keeping the focus on the audience member. It also confirms that you are carefully considering their query.

Breathe deeply during the pause to counteract any spike in nervousness and sharpen mental clarity. Send air fully into your abdomen. Exhale slowly. Even 10 seconds of deep breathing can centre you.

Use the time to quickly evaluate if you need to break a complex question down into segments before responding. Ask the speaker which aspect they would like you to address first.

For controversial questions, the pause allows emotions to settle before reacting rashly. Take time to give a thoughtful, level-headed response that acknowledges multiple perspectives.

You may also use the pause to scan your presentation notes and materials for relevant data or examples to cite. Locating these quickly strengthens your response.

If truly stumped, take a bit more time to suggest investigating the question in depth after the event. Offer to follow up with them directly with resources. Admitting some answers require research shows integrity.

As you become accustomed to speaking publicly, your ability to think on your feet will improve. With experience, you will feel more comfortable formulating extemporaneous responses. But never feel rushed into answering right away.

Even professional speakers regularly use pauses to ensure clarity. The smartest understand that gathering wisdom requires temporally distancing from the initial question. Silence sets the stage for insight.

Next time the spotlight of a Q & A produces deer-in-headlights panic, remember to breathe, reflect, and respond only when ready. Rushing produces disjointed answers.

Pausing projects presence. With poise, turn nervous energy into excitement to engage audiences authentically.

Clear and concise

When faced with audience questions after a presentation, avoid the instinct to ramble indefinitely without a clear point. Succinct, focused responses demonstrate expertise and allow more inquiries to be addressed. Prioritize clarity through brevity.

Carefully listen to each multi-faceted question, then tactfully ask the speaker which aspect they want you to focus on first. This avoids wasting time on peripheral issues they are less concerned about. Zero in on their core interest.

Frame a simple lead sentence directly answering their primary question. For example: "In terms of resources for new teachers, I would recommend our online training modules as the most accessible option." State the essence upfront.

Expand briefly with supporting details, examples or context central to the issue raised. But resist peppering responses with extraneous factoids just because you know them. Stay disciplined and targeted.

Speak in plain, easily understandable language. Avoid insider jargon and highly technical terminology if speaking to general audiences. Define any specialized vocabulary needed to address the question clearly.

Use concise phrasing and sentence structure. "The method proved inadequate for rapid scaling." Rather than, "As to the question of whether this particular methodology could have been realistically expanded at an accelerated rate, research indicates significant deficiencies."

Reference presentation slides selectively if they directly reinforce your response rather than reading long bullet points verbatim. Re-stating slide text belabours points already made.

If relevant, summarise what you covered in your presentation pertaining to the question. But avoid re-teaching whole sections. Reference back concisely without repeating the full discourse.

Remain conscious of time constraints when responding. If audiences are engaged, consider taking just 2-3 questions and thoroughly addressing them rather than skimming 10 superficially. Go deep, not broad.

If needed, propose following up later with additional details, resources or offline dialogue rather than cramming excessive minutiae into limited Q & A time. Offer your extended availability.

Close each reply with a clear summary statement circling back to the original question. For instance: "In summary, our vision emphasizes transparency, communication and accountability." Do not trail off aimlessly.

With practice, you can become adept at responding succinctly even when nervous or surprised. Take pride in distilling complex concepts into digestible sound bites without losing nuance. Less is often more.

The greater your mastery of the subject matter, the easier it becomes to address questions concisely. But stay vigilant against meandering. Crisp responses earn audience appreciation and allow richer Q & A engagement overall.

Thanks for Reading

I hope this book has proved to be useful. It is not the be all and all of public speaking and presentation skills. You should look on it as a manual for growth.

As with all things related to public speaking, experience is what makes the difference. Finding audiences to speak to and practising your craft is what will make you a great speaker.

Go to networking meetings that let you practice short pitches. Offer to speak to local businesses, chambers of commerce, schools and colleges.

Attend business seminars and conferences and see other speaker's styles. Immerse yourself as much as you can in the world of speaking. It is often said that you become the average of the people you spend most time with. If you want to be a great speaker, hang out with great speakers, or at the very least frequent the places that great speakers frequent.

www.ingramcontent.com/pod-product-compliance
Lightning Source LLC
Chambersburg PA
CBHW070930260726

48661CB00003B/924